D0580783

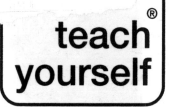

teach
yourself®

motherhood
judy reith

Launched in 1938, the **teach yourself** series grew rapidly in response to the world's wartime needs. Loved and trusted by over 50 million readers, the series has continued to respond to society's changing interests and passions and now, 70 years on, includes over 500 titles, from Arabic and Beekeeping to Yoga and Zulu. What would you like to learn?

Orders: please contact Bookpoint Ltd, 130 Milton Park, Abingdon, Oxon OX14 4SB. Telephone: +44 (0) 1235 827720. Fax: +44 (0) 1235 400454. Lines are open 09.00–17.00, Monday to Saturday, with a 24-hour message answering service. You can also order through our website www.hoddereducation.co.uk

British Library Cataloguing in Publication Data: a catalogue record for this title is available from the British Library.

First published in UK 2008 by Hodder Education, part of Hachette Livre UK, 338 Euston Road, London, NW1 3BH.

This edition published 2008.

The **teach yourself** name is a registered trade mark of Hodder Headline.

Typeset by Transet Limited, Coventry, England.
Printed in Great Britain for Hodder Education, an Hachette Livre UK Company, 338 Euston Road, London NW1 3BH, by Cox & Wyman Ltd, Reading, Berkshire.

The publisher has used its best endeavours to ensure that the URLs for external websites referred to in this book are correct and active at the time of going to press. However, the publisher and the author have no responsibility for the websites and can make no guarantee that a site will remain live or that the content will remain relevant, decent or appropriate.

Hachette Livre UK's policy is to use papers that are natural, renewable and recyclable products and made from wood grown in sustainable forests. The logging and manufacturing processes are expected to conform to the environmental regulations of the country of origin.

Impression number   10 9 8 7 6 5 4 3 2 1
Year   2012 2011 2010 2009 2008

contents

dedication

To my mother Dawn Orr, for all she said,
and all she left unsaid.

acknowledgements

I would like to thank all the mothers who have helped make this book much more interesting by being generous with their time and stories.

In addition, special thanks to my own children who are an inspiration to me everyday. My long-suffering current husband deserves an Oscar for being a mother as well as a father while I wrote this book – AWL.

You've just made a really good decision. You've got your hands on a book that will help you with the most important job you'll ever do – being a mother. Whether you're expecting your first baby and want to get ahead of the game by reading up on raising kids, or you have several children under ten, the task of motherhood is somewhere in your mind 24 hours a day, seven days a week. You might be out working every day, or maybe you're at home and not doing any kind of paid job, or perhaps you're working part time or doing voluntary work; wherever you are the world of your children is never far away. Mums are busy people running companies called families, and they're the Chief Executives largely responsible for the health, happiness and practicalities of everyone in the company. Do you have someone to share this job with? Most children are still being raised in two parent families, but all kinds of combinations of adults and children live together and if you're raising your children alone then motherhood can be ten times harder. There's not a single definition of what it is to be a mother because there are many paths along which mothers travel but whatever path you're on, this book is here to help you teach yourself more about being the kind of mother you are, and about the kind of mother you want to be. So, enjoy the journey!

Why are you reading this book?

There will be a host of different answers to this question because there are so many different kinds of mothers who are looking for reassurance or guidance, or perhaps a well-meaning friend or relative has given it to you. Generally, mothers are curious and keen to learn more about being a mother than fathers are to learn about being a father – parenting courses attract many mothers and, sadly, very few fathers. However, overall, the parenting market is booming – just look at how many parenting books and magazines are on sale today, and how Supernanny and other experts are on TV all over the world. You might have clear reasons why this book appeals to you, or maybe you're not sure at this stage what you'll get out of it. If you're hoping that this book will solve every parenting dilemma and tell you exactly what to do then the best thing you can do at this point is to give it to somebody else. It's not a 'how to' kind of book. Whatever the reasons for you now starting to read this book, you'll see that in Chapter 01 you're invited to stand back (or rather sit down and put your feet up) and take a good look at where you are now, as a mother, beginning this book. If you're pregnant with your first child, you will have more gaps to fill in about the experience of motherhood than someone who has three children under ten. Whatever your reason(s) are for choosing to make the time to read this book, you're not alone – millions of mums want to learn more about being a mum and raising kids from their birth day onwards. It makes sense. Remember, motherhood is the most important job you'll ever do.

What's the purpose of this book?

I'd like to be an ideal mother, but I'm too busy raising my kids.

Anon

There's no such thing as the perfect mother!

You'd be amazed at how many mums aim very high and feel they're not living up to their own expectations, or anyone else's. When that happens, we feel guilty, lose confidence and carry on muddling along living in a toxic environment of guilt and grumpiness. There's a whole chapter of this book devoted to being a confident mum, as lacking confidence is the number one complaint of mums everywhere. By the end of this book, if you could feel more confident as a mum, what would that be like for you? This book is written so you can teach yourself about every aspect of motherhood using techniques to help bring out the best in *you*. Create your version of being a mother, instead of just following someone else's theories.

How will you teach yourself?

You need to be curious and you need to be ready to investigate what you really want to change or learn, and how you're going to do that. You need to be specific too about setting positive, clear and realistic goals. They need to be measurable so you can see, think and feel exactly how far you've come, and how much further you need to go to reach your goals. You'll find plenty of top tips and ideas along the way to get you thinking, as well as stories from real mothers. This is your book to use in whatever way works for you. Have a good look at the contents page and see what appeals to you most. It's been written so that it doesn't matter what order you read the chapters in. As your author, I've taken the approach that most mums are too tired and busy to read pages of dense theory about being a mum. There will be theory but, more importantly, you'll be asked to make the theory come alive for *you* by completing exercises as you go. It's okay not to do the exercises, but you will learn far more about yourself if you do.

You know how you tell your children not to write in books? Well, this is a book that, by the end, will be full of your writing – ideally more than your author's!

Each chapter will end with some space for you to record your thoughts and feelings about the chapter and what you have taught yourself – if you want to. The book is written in three parts, so at the end of each section there is a learning log for you to record your achievements so far from that section of the book. There is no pressure at all to do this, but mums can benefit from recording their achievements just as much as children to signify a positive change in behaviour.

Language used in the book

Families come in all sorts of combinations and it would take far too long to write up examples of each possible combination. You will see that sometimes I use 'he' and sometimes 'she' when referring to children. Not everyone will be married or living with their children's father(s) so where appropriate I will refer to a partner and leave it up to you to interpret that accordingly. I apologize if any reader takes any offence from the language used – it certainly isn't intended.

Why should I, Judy Reith, be writing this book?

I am a professional Parent Coach, author, broadcaster and a far-from-perfect mother of three children. I found motherhood a real challenge in the early years, and by going on a parenting course I learnt the value of finding help and support. I went on to train to run courses and workshops and then qualified as a Life Coach to work one-to-one with all kinds of parents all over the world. Have a look at my website **www.parentingpeople. co.uk** to find out more about me.

I use coaching techniques and intuition to bring out the best in parents wanting to resolve parenting issues. Coaching is a positive and proactive process designed so that the client makes the changes they want or need to make. For example, a mother might be unsure about whether to go back to work or stay at home and look after her children. Or, she might have sibling rivalry issues or be facing tough decisions about schools. A Parent Coach would not resolve these issues by giving advice or telling the client what to do. Instead, the coach listens (a lot) and asks some powerful questions so that the client reaches their own conclusions. You might think you need an 'expert' to tell you what to do. In fact, by paying attention to your strengths and inner resources, as well as reading about other mums and the parenting ideas in this book, you will be in a position to generate the best solutions, tailor-made to fit your family. Imagine that.

What will be covered?

Part one – things all mums think about

Chapter 01 – *Parenting confidence*
Am I doing it right?

Mums everywhere lack confidence in their ability to raise their children. We will take a thorough look at what parenting confidence is, where it comes from, and what can take it away. Best of all, we will look at what you need to do to get your confidence flying high!

Chapter 02 – *Family values*

What is really important to you about being a mum and raising your children?

> *My partner doesn't notice if the children have bad manners, but it really matters to me and so we end up arguing about it.*

Values are what drive us and when they are ignored or belittled we get upset, so it makes sense to understand what our values are. When we have different values to our partners, friends and extended family, we need to find ways of living with these differences.

Chapter 03 – *Family relationships*

> *Is it just me who worries about how everyone is getting on?*

> *Is anyone out there having fantastic sex on a regular basis?*

Mums are in great demand by their children, their partners, their relatives, their friends and their work colleagues. It's no wonder that the energy needed to maintain all these different relationships leaves mums exhausted. This chapter will focus on taking control and boosting all these important relationships so you can turn the spotlight towards you for a change.

Part two – work or stay at home?

Chapter 04 – *Full-time mums*

> *I want to make the most of the early years looking after my children, but I feel lonely and bored sometimes.*

> *I've no idea how or when I'll get back to work and if I did, is anyone going to employ me now I'm an expert in nappies and baked beans?*

How do you make the decision to stay at home to look after your children as opposed to returning to paid employment? Chapter 04 focuses on stories from mums who have made that decision, those who have experience of being at home. You will also learn how to make the most of being at home and, when/if the time comes, how to make the transition to going back to work.

Chapter 05 – Working mums

I find myself thinking about work at home, and home at work – I'd love to be able to concentrate properly and get rid of the guilt.

All mums work, but here we're talking about mums who are paid to work, full or part time. Working mums are usually really busy and are juggling thoughts, feelings and practicalities every waking moment.

Lots of mums feel they are never quite on top of things at work or at home. This chapter will help you explore how to get the best of both worlds. Control the stress. Stop juggling. Start living.

Chapter 06 – *Taking care of you*

I want to feel great not guilty if I have some 'me' time.

Look after number one – that's you! This is probably the chapter you need to read first, but might feel like reading last. Mums have a common habit of neglecting themselves. The result is their loved ones being on the receiving end of their tiredness, irritation and lack of confidence.

This is your chance to take a good look at your priorities, and the value of putting yourself at the top of your list. What do you need to do to achieve that?

Part three – the world of children and families

Chapter 07 – *Behaviour always makes sense*

I think it's my tantrums I need to sort out more than my toddler's!

I'm sure if I could get the kids to listen to me now I might have more hope of them listening to me when they're teenagers.

What kind of mum are you? How do you deal with your children's challenging behaviour? What about sibling rivalry? These topics are all worth a book each, but this chapter will get you thinking. How will you help your children when bad stuff happens – separation, divorce, death, redundancy, bullying, tragic world news, global warming – it's a big gloomy list, but it's real life too, and a mum's job includes role modelling our response to the world we're in.

Chapter 08 – *Choosing childcare and education*

Will I ever feel completely confident in someone else's ability to look after my child?

Finding the right school – I thought giving birth was the toughest thing about having a child!

Understanding the different childcare options and what will be right for you and your child can be difficult. Settling your child when it's time for childminding or school can be anxious and stressful – how would you like it to be?

Schools – what to look for, making your mind up, and what does education mean? What is your part in your child's education?

Chapter 09 – *Running a family*

Everyone else seems to have a happy family – what's wrong with ours?

There's so much to think about on every level – practical, emotional, physical, strategic – I feel like I need to be Superwoman.

This chapter will create the chance for you to take a step back and visualize your family and how you'd like to run it. What are all the elements to family life? We will cover everything from chicken pox to chicken nuggets and ways to run the diary to help you get on top of the wonderful challenge of running a family.

Chapter 10 – *Enjoy being a mum, create a happy family*

What can I do to give my kids a happy childhood – a lot of their games are just not me?

Other mums seem to find it easy to relax and have fun with their kids; I'm always worrying about something or feel like I should be getting on with the supper.

Spending time with your children is never a 'waste of time'. In this chapter we will focus on ways to boost the fun factor and be able to step over the washing (which is a permanent feature) because you're off to have a cuddle or a game with your children.

Taking it further

My children are so young, what will I do when they're teenagers?

Where can I learn more about being a better mum?

Where were you at the start of this book and where are you now? It's time to celebrate your successes.

What do you need more of? Plus, a big list of resources such as websites, books, helplines and organizations to help you carry on teaching yourself about being a mum.

Getting started...

You will need...

A lovely pen – go on, buy the nicest one you can afford so you enjoy it every time you pick it up. This is for filling in the exercises and keeping your own notes as you teach yourself.

Next, look at the start of Chapter 01 to make your plans for reading this book so that you really know what you want to achieve by the end of it.

My promise to you...

This book will engage your imagination, and at the same time be very practical. It will motivate you to be the mum you want to be. By the end of the book you will be in a different place as a mother to the one you are in now. My hope is that you will have experienced greater confidence, organization and enjoyment of motherhood.

Your goals for reading this book

The enemies of progress are the habits that keep us comfortable just the way we are.

Anon

Having made the decision to read this book, it will help you make the most of your learning if you invest some time to fill in the questions. You can choose the order in which you read the chapters, so this is to record your intentions for learning and to give you a way of measuring your progress both at the end of any chapter, as well as at the end of the book.

Setting your goals for reading this book

When you read a recipe book and try a recipe, your goal is to see if the recipe works and the food tastes good. You have a product at the end to try and then evaluate. Motherhood is not such an exact science as cooking, but it's worth being as specific as possible about what you want to achieve from this book. What will the product be, and how will you measure its 'success?' As a mother, you might have a goal like this one:

I want my kids to be happy.

But, what does 'happy' mean? How do you know each of your children are happy? How much control do you think you have over their happiness?

A more specific and measurable version of that goal would be:

I want to make time on a regular basis to focus on what I will do to bring happiness to each of my children.

This language is specific and within the control of the goal setter. She will know she has achieved it by committing to regular times when she focuses on what *she* can do to bring happiness to her children. It could be simple things like reading them a story or cooking a meal they love, or spending some one-to-one time with the child she sees least. The point is, this mum is making progress towards bringing in more of what she wants for her children in tangible and practical ways which help her feel good about herself too. There will be more about good goal setting in Chapter 01.

Language to aim for

Have a look at the questionnaire on the next page. When you fill it in, say what you mean and mean what you say. Use phrases that are positive, specific and realistic. You might want to focus on yourself as a mother by setting a goal such as:

I want to be the best mother in the world.

The idea is lovely, but how is this measurable or specific? What are the qualities you would want to see in yourself to make you feel like you are 'the best mother in the world'? Is it patience? Kindness? Fun? Creativity? Listening? Decide what is appropriate for you. Do you see how important it is to use language that is specific, measurable, inspiring *and* within your control?

Next, it's important to work out how you will *know* you have achieved your goal. Be really clear about the differences in how you will feel, what you will be doing, thinking, seeing and hearing. Write it down or draw a picture. Say it aloud so you send a clear message to the subconscious part of your brain that you mean business.

You'll see there are some 'where are you now?' questions too, so you can see what the gap is between your current situation and where you want to get to.

Finally, it's important to record what could stop you from achieving your goals – being aware of this is the first step towards *not* letting anything stop you! You'll need about 20 minutes to complete this, so put the kettle on, find your lovely pen and ignore the phone. Most of all, do this when the children aren't around to distract you.

My goals for reading this book

1. Overall, when you finish this book, what do you want to have achieved from reading it?

2. How will you know you have achieved this?

What will you be feeling?

What will you be doing?

What will you be seeing and hearing?

What differences will those around you (children/partner) notice?

3. As this book is about teaching yourself to be a mother, rate yourself now, on a scale of 1–10 according to how satisfied you feel about your knowledge and awareness of each topic this book covers. A score of eight or more is an indicator that you already feel you know quite a lot about this subject. A score of five or less could indicate the topic you want to learn most about. Circle the number you feel applies.

Parenting confidence	1 2 3 4 5 6 7 8 9 10
Family values	1 2 3 4 5 6 7 8 9 10
Family relationships	1 2 3 4 5 6 7 8 9 10
Full-time mums	1 2 3 4 5 6 7 8 9 10
Working mums	1 2 3 4 5 6 7 8 9 10
Taking care of you	1 2 3 4 5 6 7 8 9 10
Children's behaviour	1 2 3 4 5 6 7 8 9 10
Childcare and education	1 2 3 4 5 6 7 8 9 10
Running a family	1 2 3 4 5 6 7 8 9 10
Being a fun mum	1 2 3 4 5 6 7 8 9 10

4. Looking at your lowest scoring areas, pick the three that if you could really boost your knowledge in those areas, it would have the most positive outcome on you and your family.

The areas I want to boost most are:

1.

2.

3.

For each of these areas, state specifically what you want to learn. Again, use positive, specific and measurable terms.

As a result of reading these chapters, I want to learn:

1.

2.

3.

Having acquired that knowledge, what difference would that make to you and your family?

1.

2.

3.

5. Lastly, what could stop you achieving these three goals?

6. So, what can you do to prevent this happening?

Great! You've just completed a very valuable exercise to help you determine what you want to get out of this book. Now, which chapter would you like to read first?

part one

things all mums think about

01

parenting
confidence

In this chapter you will learn:
- what is parent confidence and where it comes from
- how to boost your confidence
- the power of the F (failure) word
- how to pass confidence on to your children.

What is confidence?

Appreciate yourself for all you do and are.

Be Your Own Life Coach, Fiona Harrold

What does confidence mean to you? Someone once said it was a quiet feeling of self-worth. Gael Lindenfeld in her excellent book *Confident Teens* talks about confidence being a mixture of positive inner feelings and outer behaviour. When you feel good on the inside it's reflected on the outside. So the opposite is also true, as this mother, Tania, put it: 'I feel bombarded by so much advice and a constant nagging voice in my head that's very good at telling me what a hopeless mother I am. I'm sure that makes me behave in a hopeless kind of way towards the children.'

Confidence is unpredictable. Tania doesn't feel like this every day. Sometimes, she feels much better about herself and able to handle whatever the day throws at her. On other days, from the moment she opens her eyes until she gets to close them again (about 16 hours later) she feels that every part of her is lacking confidence. On these days she finds it all too easy to pay attention to that nagging inner critic that is so controlling and undermining.

Do you have a sense of that internal voice too? It says things like: 'You went to bed too late again', 'You had too much to drink last night', 'Your clothes are dull and you're tummy looks like a milk jelly', 'I can see your roots growing through', 'Look at the laundry basket bulging again', 'You'll never get everything done today'. And that's before you've even got out of bed, let alone encountered any children! When we pay attention to this unhelpful inner voice we feel worse about ourselves. This directly affects our ability to find the energy and frame of mind we need to be a mother. We need to tell it to shut up, and better still replace it with messages that are inspirational and spur us on, not drag us down. There will be more about that inner critic later on in this chapter.

So, inner confidence comes when we can love ourselves, feel good about ourselves and think positively, too. Think for a moment about people you would describe as confident. What is it about them that makes you think they are confident? What do they do? What do they say? How do they behave?

Confident people usually have a clear sense of purpose and direction, they are open to possibilities and adventures. They feel secure in their own self and are not dependent on others to tell them they are valuable and loved. They recognize the value of setting goals and having plans and they have a strong sense that they will achieve them, but better still, if they don't, it's not the end of the world.

What's noticeable about people who have inner confidence? They communicate effectively, speak clearly and positively. They hold their head up, their shoulders back and look you in the eye. Even if they wear shabby old clothes they still look good. They care about themselves but not in a way that you could ever describe as vain or self-centred. When life gets upsetting, difficult or out of control, confident people still maintain a sense of perspective. They respect their emotional world, but it doesn't overwhelm them. They radiate confidence.

Have a look at these quotes about confidence:

> *Whether you think you can or think you can't – you are right.*
>
> **Henry Ford**

> *If you hear a voice within you say 'you cannot paint', then by all means paint, and that voice will be silenced.*
>
> **Vincent Van Gogh**

> *I am not a has-been. I am a will be.*
>
> **Lauren Bacall**

> *Confidence comes not from always being right but from not fearing to be wrong.*
>
> **Peter T. Mcintyre**

> *Always act like you're wearing an invisible crown.*
>
> **Anon**

> *Who am I to be brilliant, gorgeous, talented, and famous? Actually, who are you not to be?*
>
> **Nelson Mandela**

It's really important to think about your confidence as a whole person because it will have a direct impact on your confidence as a parent. Sometimes mums say that they feel really confident in one part of their life such as at work, but they lack confidence at home when they are with their children.

When in your life have you felt truly confident? When have you felt on top of the world and that you're dealing well with whatever life brings?

Write here three examples from any part of your life where you have felt completely confident and had a sense of being fully alive. If you really can't think of any examples, ask family or friends if they can think of a time when they thought you were very confident. Record what happened and how you felt.

Event	My feelings
1.	
2.	
3.	

These are your real examples that mean something special to you. They prove that you *can* have that feeling of confidence. You need to believe that you'll experience fantastic feelings of confidence as a mother too if you haven't done so already.

Being a confident mum

At work, I can manage my team, handle my boss, spend my budget wisely and look amazing. I am the complete opposite at home with the children and I just can't understand why I can be so confident in one part of my life and not the other.

Angela, Accountant, two children under ten

How would you describe what confidence in a mother is?

Write it down here.

Confidence in a mother is...

How does it make you feel reading what you have written above?

My feelings are...

It could be that you feel a long way off being the confident mother you want to be. If so, you're not alone. The most common reason parents seek help with Parent Coaches is about confidence.

Being a mother involves so many parts of us – our bodies, our minds, our souls and our hearts – and then there are a million and one practical considerations as well.

> *Parents bear the responsibility of making countless daily decisions that determine whom their children have the potential to become.*

> **Hillary Rodham Clinton**

No wonder mothers all over the world find it a constant challenge to have faith that they are a 'good enough' mother. The responsibility of what we do to bring a child into the world and then nurture them through from that first mouthful of milk to seeing them leave home is the most challenging job we'll ever do. It's no surprise then that we often doubt our ability to do it. What mother wouldn't want the best for her children? What mother doesn't feel guilt and pain when she can't provide for her children, or ends up shouting and having a tantrum? What about trying to sift your way through the minefield of expertise on parenting? Everything from vaccinations to vitamins and verucas has books, websites and experts telling you what to do. Mothers everywhere want knowledge, but sometimes the search to find it is confusing and results in them feeling worse, not better, about their own ability to raise their children and their confidence takes a real knock. Motherhood is about a multitude of skills and intuition and mothers want to do the best they can... but just look at the job description.

Job title: being a mother

WANTED

VOLUNTEER

For the most important job in the world

Would suit person with the following skills:

Teaching, cooking, running a household, nursing, sorting out arguments, solving all kinds of problems, giving advice, having eyes in the back of your head, juggling many different things at once.

Applicants must be committed, flexible and patient, have energy, a sense of humour, an overdraft facility, and an understanding of children at different ages and stages.

Night shifts are part of the job.

No qualifications necessary. No training given but ample opportunity to learn on the job.

Rest days: nil

Renumeration: nil

Promotion prospects: low

Minimum length of service: 18 years.

It makes your head spin just thinking about it!

With a job description like that, does it surprise you that you're bound to have days when it all gets too much and you feel like the worst mother in the world? You feel guilty, bewildered and probably exhausted too, and so you tell yourself you're not very good at it.

We could carry on looking at the reality of motherhood and how it zaps your confidence, but it would probably be more helpful to have an MOT, like cars do, about your own levels of motherhood confidence at this point.

It's helpful to break down where you are feeling most and least confident. Take a look at the chart below and complete this exercise.

(We know that confidence blows up and down, so try to answer these questions according to how you feel generally rather than specifically today.)

Let's start with our inner confidence:

Look at the list of common inner feelings and thoughts which mothers have that affects their confidence. Consider how often you feel this way and tick the box that applies. Tick the negative thoughts with a red pen and the positive ones with a green pen.

Feelings/thoughts	Every day	Weekly	Rarely	Never
Low self-respect				
High self-respect				
I am a bad mother				
I am a good mother				
I am a good enough mother				
I feel unsure about being a mother				
I love being a mother				
I am confused about what I think about motherhood				
I have clear ideas about motherhood				
I think positively about motherhood				
I think negatively about motherhood				
I feel I can cope as a mother				
I don't feel I can cope as a mother				
I feel other mothers are better than me				

	Every day	Weekly	Rarely	Never
I feel I'm just as good a mother as my friends/my own mum				
Add your own feelings here if they're missing from the list.				

What do you notice about your ticks? Any patterns or surprises?

Which feelings would you like to have more of and by how much?

For example, if you ticked 'rarely' for the statement 'I think positively about motherhood', and you want to think like that much more often, you could rewrite it as 'I want think positively about motherhood everyday'. Notice the word 'want'. When we say what we want, we are much more likely to find ways to meet that desire. It is a positive and constructive frame of mind to adopt rather than saying what we don't want.

I want to feel or think more… (and how often)

If you had sound inner confident feelings about motherhood what would that be like for you? What would that be like for your children? What differences would they see in you?

External confidence

Meet Suzie. She is a fictitious mother who is full of confidence on the inside and it shows in her behaviour and her communication. Have a look at what Suzie is like, and think about whether you are like that and if so, how often.

Suzie	You			
	Every day	Weekly	Rarely	Never
Cares about what she eats				
Watches her alcohol				
Makes sure she catches up on sleep				
Takes pride in her appearance				
Takes regular exercise				
Makes time for herself				
Makes time for the relationships she cares about				
Knows what she is good at				
Makes clear plans and carries them through				
Leaps out of bed in the morning				
Smiles a lot				
Has energy for her children				
Talks about how much she loves them				
Shows how much she loves them				
Looks for the good in them and other people				
Talks positively and optimistically				
Listens carefully				
Negotiates calmly				
Controls her temper when frustrated				
Motivates herself when she hits a rough patch				
Takes pride in her home				
Is a pleasure to be with				

Does Suzie really exist? Who is this Supermum? There is no such thing as a perfect mother. Suzie's qualities are there to inspire you not depress you. No doubt you're doing the best you can as a mother and there are times when you can be more like Suzie and times when it's a miracle just to get through the day without walking out or guzzling vodka.

When you look down your frequency list how often are you like Suzie? Which features on Suzie's list would you like more of? What is it about those features that make them significant? Pick the top eight that, if you could do something about them, would have the biggest impact on your confidence as a mother. Has this got you thinking and have you thought of other features about being a confident mother that you would like to add to this list?

The point is, what would be significant for you? What would make a positive difference to your confidence levels?

Boost my confidence wheel

Think of eight features that would help to increase your confidence and write each of these in a section of the wheel below.

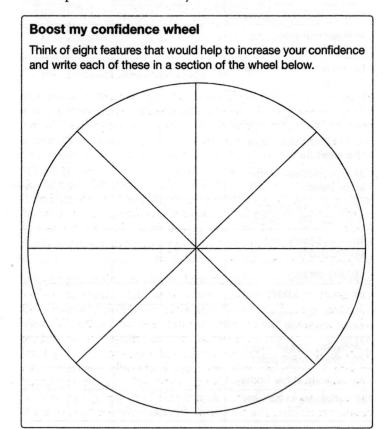

Now, identify an action that could be achievable, positive and within your control that you could do in the coming week to really boost your confidence as a mum. Write it down beside the appropriate section of the wheel and then **put it in your diary.** That's to give it the best chance of success. An action needs to have a time set aside for it so it's much more likely to happen. One mum wanted to get more sleep so she committed to going to bed 15 minutes earlier each night. Another decided to think more positively about her children so she wrote down five things she loved about them at the end of each day. She also put some lovely photos of them in her wallet. You decide. What will you do this week and when?

Your strengths as a mother

It's about recognizing the significance of what you do in the mundane details. Run the bathwater or spread the peanut butter and proclaim loudly 'I'm making my contribution to the future of the planet!'

Joyce Maynard, *Mother's Wit*

Mothers are notoriously good at putting themselves down and telling themselves and anyone else listening what they are *not* good at. You hear it everywhere. They say things like 'I'm no good at dealing with tantrums', 'I haven't got any time to cook a proper meal', 'I haven't got a clue how to deal with homework', 'I don't mind shopping for the children but I hate shopping for me'. Or, perhaps worst of all, 'I'm only a mum'. All this adds up to powerful feelings of failure, or the F word for short. The F word is nearly as harmful to a mother's confidence as the G word (guilt). There is nothing to be gained from allowing feelings of failure to keep their grip on you. Failure is not an option so don't tell yourself you're a failure as a mother.

A mother's negativity can be endless and it isn't doing anyone any good at all. It usually stems from high standards we set ourselves as mothers, sometimes based on our own mothers and what they were like or other mothers around us. But, it's very important to focus on the simple everyday things you do and see them as strengths. One mum who did this found it very hard initially to come up with anything. Eventually she recognized that even thinking about this was a strength in itself. It showed she cared and that depth of care will keep her going, and of course her children, all their lives. No one says you have to wash their clothes or read them a story or organize 40 extra curricular activities. Their lives *don't* depend on a whole host of things we do, but we choose to do them because we want to do the best we can.

So, what are your strengths as a mother?

What do you do well? What aspects do you find easy and enjoyable?

One mum, Jenny, said 'I had three sons then a daughter and at last I could have great fun adding fairy dresses and tiaras to the dressing-up box.'

We often find it easier to recognize the qualities we admire in others, including our children, but it's time to pat yourself on the back. Use the space below to fill in what you do well as a mother and keep it somewhere you can see it easily and add to it as your children grow older. If you find this really tough why not ask your partner and your children what they would say your strengths are?

What are my strengths as a mother?

(e.g. I make time to play, I cook them a favourite meal)

When we appreciate what we do, we will find it easier to appreciate our children. It's far better for our children to hear us talk about what we do well too. It's not boasting, it's affirming your strengths as a mother.

What or who knocks your confidence?

We know that we all have good days and bad days, or parts of our life where we feel really confident and other parts where we don't. To keep our confidence up we must recognize what knocks it. Who or what is causing us to wobble? Mothers are very good at talking negatively about all the things we don't do, or about our negative feelings – so we are the most likely cause of challenges to our confidence. We need to re-invent our view of ourselves and do everyone a favour, especially our children. Once we take control of our own thoughts and feelings about ourselves, we will find it much easier to deal with the other factors that affect our confidence. Apart from our own ability to knock ourselves and damage our confidence, there are a number of other key players in this role. We will examine who these people are once we have had a good look at the part we play first.

Your beliefs about yourself as a mother

What you believe about yourself as a mother has a direct impact on your children. It might sound obvious, but so often we allow our negative beliefs about ourselves to control us. Negative beliefs produce harmful self-talk which encourages you to behave, think and feel accordingly.

You can choose to pay attention to those beliefs, or you can decide, from today, that you're going to banish them and replace them with positive ones instead. What have you got to lose but old unhelpful beliefs about yourself that create thoughts, feelings and behaviours that are no good for you, or your children, or your partner, if you have one.

Start here...

You should have just finished writing down lots of positive strengths you have as a mother. Next, write down all the negative beliefs you hold about yourself as a mother.

What are my weaknesses as a mother?

(e.g. I am a lazy mum, I am always tired, I am extremely disorganized)

Decide which beliefs are the ones that really hold you back and choose the top three. Write them here.

Where did these beliefs come from?

Who gave them to me?

Are these beliefs actually true?

What is it costing me to hold on to these beliefs on a daily basis?

What would I be capable of as a mother if I could let go of these beliefs?

Now, go back to the beginning of the box where you wrote in your negative beliefs about yourself as a mother and reread them. Then, go to the box on page 17 and rewrite your negative beliefs as positive ones. Use clean and simple language. That will send a very strong message to the subconscious part of your brain, which will help you act on your new beliefs.

> **My new beliefs about myself as a mother**
>
> (e.g. I am an energetic mother [instead of a lazy one])

Say these beliefs out loud now.

Finally, find a red pen and go back to that first box where you wrote in your negative beliefs and put a red line diagonally through them and write DELETE. You're not going to let those beliefs have their power over you any more. If they creep in, then immediately replace them with the positive one you've identified in the box above.

This may sound far too simple, but many people have completed this exercise and found it has made a tremendous difference to them.

> *I was always telling myself I was disorganized and finding evidence to back that up. Having completed this exercise and re-written that belief as 'I am organized' it's made such a difference. The 'Confidence wheel' and timetabled actions from that actually works, and I've already got next year's diary! I feel much better.*
>
> Rebecca, working mum with three children under ten

Look at your new beliefs and make sure you can say them aloud regularly to reinforce their message. You have updated what you believe about yourself as a mother, and your subconscious mind will be looking for evidence to support these new beliefs. It's a bit like having a good clear-out at home. You create space and feel so much better with it. In that space, you choose to put the things that you enjoy, things that are good for you and enable you to function well and thrive. Notice the difference in yourself now as you read and say these beliefs and be encouraged that you CAN control what you believe about yourself. Note down any differences you observe in your thoughts, feelings and actions at the end of this chapter.

Who else interferes with your confidence?

The mother-in-law frequently forgets that she was a daughter-in-law.

Anon

It's natural that we pay attention to what other people say about us, but how much is it affecting our confidence as mothers? Strong confidence comes from within. If you are over-dependent on other people telling you that you are doing a good job as a mother, then it's likely that your confidence will be unstable. Of course, if people pay you compliments then it's a great boost, but deep down you need to feel just fine as you are, without having to be told so by others. Your confidence needs to be within your control. For the same reason, you need to stay strong when critical comments or looks come your way from other influential people in your life. It's not that these people *intend* to put you down, it's just that they have control and power over you, especially when you value their opinion. However, is that how you want it to stay?

It's helpful to identify who these people are that influence your confidence levels. One mum had on her list: my childminder, my health visitor, my mum, my older sister, my mother-in-law, my ante-natal mums, my husband, my boss.

Who would be on your list?

Who interferes with my confidence?

Consider in detail what they are actually saying or doing. For example, is your childminder saying or implying that your children are badly behaved? If she's actually saying so, then what can you do to put that right? Or is it in your imagination? Sophie, a mother of two, assumed her childminder disapproved of her because she worked full time, but when she thought about it rationally, that's exactly what the childminder did too!

Perhaps your mother-in-law is disapproving of you feeding her grandchildren fish fingers? What would you like to be able to say to her that would be positive and constructive? In other words, taking each example of someone who is denting your confidence, how could you view what's going on differently so it doesn't dent your confidence? It's a bit like being inside and someone knocking at the door. You can see them from an upstairs window, but they don't know if you're there or not. You can choose whether to let them in or let them think nobody is home.

> **Top tip**
> The world is full of unasked-for advice. You choose what you pay attention to, what you listen to and what you act on.

Creating confident children

This book is written to help you teach yourself motherhood, but it would be a shame in a chapter about confidence to not include a quick guide about the value of creating confidence in your children. It's widely known that confident children achieve more at school, are able to integrate in all kinds of situations and are popular with other children and adults. Who wouldn't want a child like that? Like adults, children's confidence goes up and down, and it can vary in different parts of their life too. You might have a child who is full of beans at school, but when they go to football or ballet they are shy and reluctant to join in. But, overall, do your children feel that they are capable? Do they have a deep understanding that they are loved, which in turn gives them the security to love and then go and take on the world?

In previous generations, confident children may have been labelled as 'show offs' or 'full of themselves'. So many of today's parents are trying to find the balance between encouraging confidence without producing a child that will be a pain to everyone else. Again, it can be the grandparents who can undermine the confidence of our children, as Jane, a mother with three children put it, 'I dread taking the kids to visit my parents as Dad thinks the children are far too bold and he doesn't hesitate to put them in their place.'

Teachers too, have a very powerful part to play in boosting or reducing children's confidence. How many adults can you think of who say things like, 'My music teacher told me I couldn't sing', and they still don't sing, or paint, or think they can do maths or climb a rope – the list is endless. Adults everywhere are still living without experiencing many things in their lives because a teacher in their childhood managed to undermine their confidence in that area. If you hear of or overhear anything being said to your children in school that is damaging their confidence, do take action. Show your child that you believe they are capable of having a go at anything.

> *At my school, some teachers call me Little Tessie, rather than by my own name, because my older sister is called Tessie. She is really clever and I'm not.*

> Lucy, nine years old

Our children's friends are another major factor affecting their confidence. Children can be so cruel to each other and say unspeakable things that we find very hard to forget. That old saying 'Sticks and stones may break my bones but names will never hurt me' is rubbish. Children using violence on each other is wrong, but ask any adult who was labelled 'fat' or 'thick' by their childhood contemporaries if those names don't still hurt and stick with them.

I could write a whole book about bullying, and you can find some useful websites in the Taking it further section if you need them. The most important thing is to take bullying seriously and also alert the school and find out what their policy is on it. Make sure your child feels supported by you – don't let home become another battleground when they're having a hard time at school.

So what can mums (and dads) do to build confidence in their children so they feel lovable and capable?

Let your child take risks

This is age appropriate, but find ways to help them explore and discover their own limits – climb fences and trees, learn to use scissors or a knife for cutting vegetables, ride a bike.

Encourage them to make decisions and take on responsibility

Allow them to choose what they wear or make them responsible for looking after their possessions. Agree which clothes are for school or special occasions. It's easy to fall into the trap of being the fixer and sorter when something goes wrong.

My son was always forgetting his P.E. kit and I would take it into school for him. I decided it was time he took responsibility and it was really hard not to run after my son but he learnt his lesson and he hasn't forgotten it since.

Janice, mum of nine-year-old

Let children do what they're capable of doing and review this regularly – e.g. washing, dressing, helping round the house, running errands. It also provides lots of opportunities to praise them for their efforts.

Give some choices

This is about being wise with the language you use and the age of the children. For example, saying to a child under five 'What do you want for supper?' can be confusing to them, but giving them a choice between two things, such as baked potato or pasta allows them to feel they have had some choice.

Listen, listen, listen

One of the best ways to help boost their confidence is to listen and say not very much at all. They may be used to you constantly 'fixing' their grievances and offering advice, but by just listening there is a very good chance they will come to their own conclusion about what they want to do. Then they feel so much better that they have solved the problem themselves.

Respect feelings

When our children show strong feelings like crying, laughing too loudly or being over-excited, we're tempted to squash those feelings and deny the strength of them. It's much more helpful to children to have their feelings acknowledged. Describe what you see. For example, if they're screaming after a fall, what would comfort them more, 'Don't be silly, it's not that bad' or 'Ouch, I bet that hurt'. If the feelings are acknowledged, then the child is on the way to being able to manage them. They will feel heard and understood, which boosts their confidence.

Setting boundaries

All these ideas will be covered in more detail in Chapter 07 on children's behaviour, but the link here with confidence is worth noting. Are you constantly being critical about how they eat, look after their possessions and behave? Is your household full of rules 'Don't do this, don't do that'. How much can you tolerate and let them learn for themselves and how many boundaries do you need to set? Involve them in setting boundaries. Ask them what they think is reasonable; their answers could surprise and delight you.

Language

What we say and how we say it has a very big impact on our children because we are the most powerful people in their lives. Mothers are experts at noticing when their children are going 'wrong' and are very quick to point it out. 'Don't leave your shoes there', 'You never do what I ask', 'Don't speak like that to me'.

We ignore the large chunks of time when things are going OK or even really well. A good first step in boosting their confidence is to decide to comment on when they do something right (like hang up a coat, or say thank you) and ignore anything else unless it's a real emergency and someone is about to get hurt. Better still, say far more of what you *do* want them to do rather than what you don't.

Top tip

Give up saying **don't** and replace it with more **do's**.

List here your own daily gripes you have with your children such as: 'Don't be so noisy'. Then rewrite what you normally say using positive language that communicates what you want to happen.

What I say now	How I can say it positively
e.g. Don't be so noisy	I want you to be quiet

Love them

Remember, in order to love and appreciate our children, we need to do that for ourselves first. Turn back and reread what you wrote earlier in this chapter about your strengths as a mother.

Now, think about your children. Think about how much you love them. Think about their unique qualities and what you appreciate in them. Write them below.

We will end here with you looking at this list of everything you love and appreciate about your children. What better way to close the chapter on confidence?

What I love and appreciate about my child(ren) (their name)

Learning log

Check you are happy that you have learnt each point below and feel ready to apply it to your life.

- What confidence is.
- What confidence means for mothers and for me.
- How to boost my confidence.
- My strengths as a mother.
- Who interferes with my confidence?
- My beliefs about myself as a mother.
- How to raise confident children.

What have I learnt about myself as a mother by reading this chapter?

What is the most significant thing?

02

family values

In this chapter you will learn:

- what are values and where they come from
- the links between values and behaviour
- how other people's values impact on you
- about passing values on to children.

*I never went to school beyond the third grade, but my
mother taught me the difference between right and wrong.*

Joe Lewis, from *Mother's Wit*

What are values?

Values are what you think is good or bad, right or wrong,
desirable or undesirable. Not only do you think about values,
they inform how you behave and communicate all the time. They
are the standards and qualities by which you live your life. When
you are a mother, they are likely to be the standards that you are
raising your children to meet. They are internal qualities that you
think are important like truth, love, honesty, respect and
kindness – qualities abundant with meaning to us.

They are represented externally by how we behave. So, for
example, if love is one of your core values, you will be
consciously and subconsciously including expressions of love in
your life. When it is missing or unsatisfactory, you find it
upsetting. Similarly, if honesty is really important to you and
you discover your child is lying to you, this will be upsetting. A
parent less concerned with honesty would not necessarily be so
upset. When you find yourself angry and wanting to make sure
your child sees the error of their ways it's likely to be because a
value of yours has been trodden on.

Your values are the qualities that are really important to you; it's
as simple as that.

What do you think your values are? Here are some ideas to get
you thinking, taken from Linda Kavelin Popov's book *The
Family Virtues Guide.*

Assertiveness	Kindness
Caring	Love
Cleanliness	Loyalty
Compassion	Mercy
Confidence	Moderation
Consideration	Modesty
Courage	Obedience
Courtesy	Orderliness
Creativity	Patience
Detachment	Peacefulness

Determination	Purposefulness
Enthusiasm	Reliability
Excellence	Respect
Faithfulness	Responsibility
Flexibility	Reverence
Forgiveness	Self- Discipline
Friendliness	Service
Generosity	Steadfastness
Gentleness	Tact
Helpfulness	Thankfulness
Honesty	Tolerance
Honour	Trust
Humility	Trustworthiness
Idealism	Truthfulness
Joyfulness	Unity
Justice	

Where do values come from?

Mother always said that honesty was the best policy and money isn't everything. She was wrong about other things too.

Gerald Brazen, *Mother's Wit*

So, where do values come from? One guess... yes, your parents. Not all your values, but the core values that are central to what you think is the right or wrong way to live your life. These values are formed in us from a very early age. Our parents talking to us from day one is partly how we pick up their values, but they become even more engraved on our hearts and minds by observing how our parents behave. Other major factors in forming our own values are education and religion. A teacher might have captured our imagination with their passion for their subject and we may find ourselves anxious if one of our children has a bad experience with a teacher in that same subject. Or, we might have been yelled at for having untidy handwriting, so we find ourselves insisting that our children's handwriting is neat and tidy – we don't want them to be yelled at like we were. All the major world religions instil in their followers a moral code to live by. For many, trying to work out what's right or wrong, important or unimportant, is helped by practising their faith. Most religions offer a handbook to live by – some people find this makes their life more straightforward as they believe in a clear set of rules to live by.

Religion and teachers and other influential adults in early childhood all play their part in shaping our value system. However, most of us probably still took more notice, consciously or unconsciously, of how our parents lived their lives.

We watched our mothers cleaning and tidying – we sensed it was important to her to keep the home that way. We noticed our father get angry if we were cheeky – it was important to him that his children spoke to him politely, being cheeky showed a lack of respect. Perhaps there was very little love on show – we got the message that it wasn't that important to our parents to be affectionate. For some, the values we grew up with had a detrimental effect on us, so the opposite values become important to us when we're raising our own children.

Mum's thoughts on values

My values for bringing up my children are all born out of what I experienced as a child. My number one value is to create warmth and love for my children because my parents were cold and unloving. I'm sure they didn't mean to be, they just were. Also, I want my children to feel it's okay to talk about their feelings, because it was definitely not okay for me to talk about mine as a child – it still isn't.

Ellie, two children, seven and five years old

As children grow older and spend time in other people's families, they become aware of how other families have different values. They might decide to adopt them for themselves.

I used to love going round to my friend's house because they played games all the time as a family. Having fun together was important and very natural to them: the opposite was true in our house.

Tania, three daughters, all under 12 years old

It's also true that we can appreciate the values our parents had and wish to pass these on to our children.

My parents valued honesty more than anything else and although it was tough at times, especially when we were teenagers, I think they were right. Being around dishonesty always makes me feel uncomfortable and I think that's a good thing.

Angela, three children under 12 years old

Thinking back to your own childhood, answer this question:

In the family I grew up in, it was important to...

1.

2.

3.

4.

5.

6.

7.

8.

9.

10.

(You might find it helpful to have a look at the list of values again at the beginning of this chapter.)

In the same family there can be big differences in what's important according to the position, gender, age and personality of the family members. Your brothers or sisters might have grown up in the same house as you, but their values could be different to yours. One person might regard keeping healthy as a value for them, so they take regular exercise and watch their diet. However, their sibling might not see this as important at all, they may be quite happy to live off donuts and the idea of exercise may not enter their head. If you have siblings, what do you imagine they would have written in the box above and how would their answers be different to yours?

Parenting values are partly influenced by the character of parent too. You might have had a very strict mother and an open and relaxed father. On the surface, it would be easy to suggest that the mother had more values than the father but she probably just expressed them more than he did. Perhaps it was more important to her than to him to create rules and make sure they were obeyed.

Remember: Parents having different values is a common source of conflict in families – more about this later.

The impact of values on plans and actions

Think about your typical day and consider how many of your plans and actions are driven by your values. We fill our diary and our children's diaries (and our partner's too!) with a range of actions because we think they're important. Nobody tells us we must take our children to football, ballet and piano lessons but many mothers do these things because they think it's important to expand their children's education. It might be because they think exercise is important or perhaps their own parents placed a high value on extra-curricular activities. We make social arrangements based on our values. We make decisions about spending money on everything from buying everyday groceries to washing machines based on values. We decide about our leisure time, our health needs and our hobbies because our values are driving us. So, we have a list of values (what's important to us) in all the major areas of our life, and these can blur into what we think is important as a mother. In the next chapter, which focuses on family relationships, we will explore further the impact of this on our family dynamics.

Can values change?

Yes, is the short answer. You're unlikely to change your core values, but it is possible to add on more values. Our knowledge and awareness increases and our priorities change, so what used to be unimportant becomes important. Jackie is a great example of this: 'I really didn't think it was very important to recycle our rubbish, before I had children but now it's hugely important to me as I'm much more aware of environmental issues. I get very irritated when the children throw things in the bin that can be recycled.'

For mothers, adding on more values or prioritizing them differently is part of adapting to different needs as children grow up, their personalities develop or circumstances change. A mother with a young toddler will probably have safety high up on her list of values whereas a mother with an eight year old would still regard safety as very important, but education could feel more important at this stage. By the time the child is a teenager, safety could well be top of her agenda again!

For the first two years of being a mother, it never crossed my mind to be concerned about the Internet and how my child would use it. But now he's nine I think it's really important to take technology seriously and be up to date with it as the Internet is a useful tool, but children need to use it wisely.

Jackie, two children under ten years old

Values in relationships

Values are represented differently according to the context they are in. For example, your values about relationships such as trust, honesty, or commitment may be different to your values about work which could be creativity, financial rewards, ethics etc. Life events such as separation, divorce and bereavement can also cause a shift in our values and how we might prioritize them. A divorcing mother may find that happiness is now her number one value as her children have been exposed to a lot of unhappiness as a result of the divorce. Prior to divorce, it's possible that a very different value was top of her list, such as love, health or education. We are mothers, but we're also daughters, and maybe sisters, wives or partners, aunts, neighbours, friends, employers or employees, and our values could be listed differently for all these relationships.

Are beliefs the same thing?

Beliefs are different, but they do create rules that we live our lives by, which is similar to the effect our values have on us. A belief is something we consider to be true about ourselves and because we hold this belief, it affects the way we think and behave. We believe positive and negative things about ourselves as we noted in the previous chapter about confidence. On the negative side, we might believe we're lazy, incompetent, selfish or no good at maths. We can hold positive beliefs too, such as considering ourselves happy, confident or considerate. We might have a value as a mother that it's important *to be* considerate, but that's not the same as believing you *are* a considerate person. What we believe shapes the way we see the world and impacts on our behaviour. Negative beliefs limit our potential and need to be reclaimed as positive beliefs so we can thrive.

Go back to the beliefs exercise in the Chapter 01 'Your beliefs about yourself as a mother' and check you have really understood how important it is to be aware of the power of negative beliefs and the value of challenging them, and the freedom and potential of harbouring positive ones.

When you update your beliefs you instruct your unconscious mind on how things are going to be from now on.

Jeff Archer, Life Coach

You may already know your values about being a mother or a parent, but the following exercise will help you determine and prioritize them. When our values are ignored or trampled on, we are not honouring them; subsequently, we feel upset and behave accordingly.

Parenting values

What values are really important to you as a parent?

It could be values like being kind, fun, wise, patient, creative, sporty or controlling. A clue to identifying your values can be finding out what upsets you. For example, losing your temper may make you feel distressed; or if being fun is important, you may find it difficult when you haven't got the energy to be fun. Write them down in the box below – aim for about ten values that are important to you.

Consider how much each value is being honoured or respected in your life? On a scale of 1–10 (1 being no respect, and 10 being perfect with no room for improvement) circle the number you feel is right for you.

Values as a mother	Current score
1.	1 2 3 4 5 6 7 8 9 10
2.	1 2 3 4 5 6 7 8 9 10
3.	1 2 3 4 5 6 7 8 9 10
4	1 2 3 4 5 6 7 8 9 10
5.	1 2 3 4 5 6 7 8 9 10
6.	1 2 3 4 5 6 7 8 9 10
7.	1 2 3 4 5 6 7 8 9 10
8.	1 2 3 4 5 6 7 8 9 10
9.	1 2 3 4 5 6 7 8 9 10
10.	1 2 3 4 5 6 7 8 9 10

A score of less than six means this part of your life needs some attention if you want to feel more content as a mother.

Now try to put your ten values in order of what is the most important to you. What jumps out at you? If you're not sure, put each value up against each other. For example, if you could have trust, but no fun, which would you keep? Keep doing this until you are really satisfied that you have them in order of importance to you.

What are your top three? Write them in the box below. These are your core values and when they are trampled on, you are most likely to feel upset, fearful, disappointed, angry, or frustrated.

My top three core values as a mother...

1.

2.

3.

Write next to them the current score you gave them for being respected in your life.

One mum Hannah said:

> *Having completed this exercise I can see now why I get so upset about the children fighting. It is really important to me that they get on well and the house is calm. I'm fairly certain this stems from my own childhood as my older siblings were always fighting and it made my mum so cross, which I hated. So, when my children fight I will do anything to stop it and intervene whereas my husband doesn't even seem to notice until there's blood on the carpet! As a result they expect* me *to intervene and sort it out so I guess I am adding to the problem.*

What are the behaviours and feelings you can identify when you know your core parenting values are not being respected?

Value	Behaviour	Feelings
e.g. Respect	Nagging my kids about helping out	Resentment, anger
1.		
2.		
3.		

Now, to make this practical and real, identify some common examples in your family life that you find challenging that could be down to your values being ignored. Aim for about ten.

What you see/hear	Value	My behaviour
1. e.g. Untidy bedrooms	Tidiness or control	I nag and shout
2.		
3.		
4.		
5.		
6.		
7.		
8.		
9.		
10.		

Values create behaviour

The list you have created on page 34 is to help you understand how values impact on your behaviour as a mother. Bear in mind that values are not the only reasons we behave as we do. An untidy room could also make you nag and shout because you're really tired or pre-menstrual that day. Or it could be a one-off event, you might be expecting visitors and have a value about being concerned about what they will think of you or the children if their rooms are untidy. This is about raising your awareness about general patterns of your behaviour so you can create an opportunity to do something differently. Exploding for no apparent reason can often mean a value has been trampled on. We can suddenly react to something and be out of control which is distressing for both our children and us. We might not understand where the behaviour has come from, but it will have a root somewhere, and it could well be a value has been ignored or disrespected.

Behaviour always makes sense.

Tony Humphries, Irish psychologist

A perfect example of how understanding your values can influence your behaviour is seen in Linda. She spent some time thinking about her core values as a mother and concluded that they were love, then protection, then happiness. She realized that she was fed up with telling her daughter she had too much housework to do, so there wasn't time to play with her. This meant that Linda had a value about the house being tidy, but she identified that it was more important to make time to show her daughter she loved her by ignoring the housework when she got home from school and playing with her instead. They both felt much happier, which met another of Linda's values as a mother.

Other people's values

Having different values are a common source of family conflict. Understanding this will help you to manage conflict better, and to aim for respect, tolerance and patience on both sides. We know that our values are likely to come from our parents. It takes a lot of effort trying to maintain those values or discard them now we have our own children to raise. When we're choosing our life partner, we are more likely to talk about where to live and work, and how much we love each other, rather than about the values we'll instil in any children we produce. Consider other people's values – whose have the biggest impact on you as a mother? Is it your husband or partner? Is it your own parents or his parents? Is it your friends or siblings? Put them in the wheel below.

Other people's values affecting me

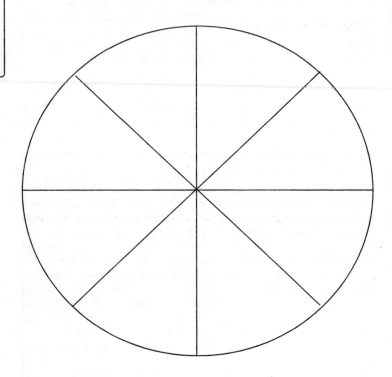

Which other person's values have the biggest negative impact on you as a mother?

What are the circumstances or examples that have led you to select this person? Your examples might seem like small things such as using a butter knife or big things like your husband having a strong opinion that your children must go to private school whereas you may be keen on state education. When you clash, it creates ill feeling, tension, resentment and rows.

Minor values clash (e.g. butter knife)

1.

2.

3.

Major values clash (e.g. education)

1.

2.

3.

How would your life be different if you could resolve the clash of values between you and this person?

List five positive differences here and write in the first person. For example, if you could resolve the butter knife dispute with your husband you would feel happier at breakfast and more relaxed, write 'I would feel happier at breakfast and more relaxed'.

1. I would…

2.

3.

4.

5.

We often put up with these kinds of spoken and unspoken tensions and struggles for years and they can be extremely harmful to us and to our children.

> **Top tip**
>
> Make time with your partner to talk about, appreciate and understand your different parenting values. If you are no longer a couple this can be hard, but persevere!

It's a really good idea to use this opportunity to notice the impact of value-clashing in your significant relationships, and to note why it would be worth doing something about it. We will cover this in more detail in Chapter 03, which is all about family relationships. For now, think of five ways in which you could do something about these clashes, like Sarah did:

I was really fed up with having to go to my in-laws every year for Christmas and I knew my husband was reluctant to stand up to his mother and tell her we wanted to have Christmas at our house. I felt it was important to start creating our own traditions, and deep down my husband agreed, so one night we sat down and I explained my feelings to him and asked for his support to decide what we could do. I was prepared to talk to his mum, but in the end he told her, and at the same time invited her and his dad to come to our house for Christmas Day instead. She was a bit upset, but my husband didn't waiver and suggested she could bring the pudding. It was a good day; my mother-in-law was a bit uneasy, but after a sherry or two she was fine and I made sure I had plenty of jobs to keep her busy. It's such a relief to have broken that pattern and my husband is much happier about it too.

Before you fill in the box on page 39, go and find your diary.

What can I do this week about value clashes that affect me as a mother?	
What I will think, do or say (e.g. see a butter knife as a good idea)	**When** From tomorrow
1.	
2.	
3.	
4.	
5.	

Passing on values to our children

Children are the sum of what mothers contribute to their lives.

Anon

Our children are born like a blank canvas waiting for their parents to pick up the brush and start filling in the patterns, shapes and colours of their lives. The science world is endlessly debating if the parents *are* painting the entire picture, or if some of it has already been painted before the child is born. The nature/nurture debate goes on because who can really say what is there before the child is born? Studies of twins have shown that two children born at the same time can have completely different personalities and behaviours despite the parents claiming to have nurtured them in exactly the same way. Other studies have shown that even with twins born minutes apart, the parents still treat the first twin as the oldest and have different expectations of them and even call the younger twin 'the baby'. Parents are the single most powerful influence on how children turn out as adults, and a significant part of this is how parents pass on what they think is right and wrong, as demonstrated through their value system.

Sometimes our children are left in no doubt about what we value as we say it ten times a day. In addition, our parent's values come to us through more abstract routes. We simply sense their approval or disapproval through a fleeting glance or a barely audible sigh.

My parents never said anything directly to me, but I just knew they would be hugely disappointed if I lost my virginity before my wedding night.

Stuart, married with three children

However, if we neglect to explain to our children the difference between what is right and wrong as we see it, then society and their friends (and we, and they) will have to live with the consequences. This is especially true in the adolescent years, which are not covered in this book. We are fed on a diet of our parents' values from the moment we are born. So, passing on our values needs to have a considered approach. We must live them, not just talk about them. That old saying 'Do as I say, not as I do' does not carry much weight with children. They are watching us all the time, and our words won't mean much to them if they don't match up with our actions. As one couple put it: 'We were always asking our children to hang up their clothes and one day it occurred to us that we never hung up our clothes, so was it reasonable to expect them to hang up theirs?'

If you feel this is true for you, it might be helpful here to identify the most common areas where you feel you say one thing and do another – sending a mixed message to your children.

It's natural to want or expect more from our children than to see them going through life tolerating what we tolerate. Knowing you have struggled to live with your own self-doubts for years is a big motivator to stopping your children when you think they are being like you. But, our children are unique individuals and may not turn out like us. The best thing we can aim for is to live out our values in such a way that makes sense of who we are. We need to be open to the idea of adding on values as our children change. Doing this will help your children to respect you and you will feel true to yourself.

What I say e.g. Tell them they have to eat breakfast	What I do Don't eat breakfast myself
1.	
2.	
3.	
4.	
5.	

Children watch the way their parents live their lives. If they like what they see, if it makes sense to them, they will live their lives that way too.

Colin Powell from *The Language of Parenting*

Learning log

Check you are happy that you have learnt each point below and feel ready to apply it to your life.

- What are values and where do they come from?
- The links between our values and our behaviour.
- How to identify your values as a mother.
- Other people's values that impact on you.
- How to pass on your values to your children.

What have I learnt about myself as a mother by reading this chapter?

What is the most significant thing?

03 family relationships

In this chapter you will learn:
- how to evaluate relationships
- how to create a family vision
- what style of mother you are
- to make time for your partner.

Nobody's family can hang out the sign 'Nothing's the matter here'.

Chinese proverb

Why family relationships matter to mums

Case study: Kate

6.30 a.m. and the alarm goes off and you need to get up before waking the children if the day is to get off to a good start. Your two year old is beside you spread eagled. He arrived in your bed in the early hours after you had helped him with a vomiting episode and you were just too tired to take him back to his own bed. Your husband Jim is in the shower and is probably disgruntled that his wandering hands on you last night had once again been rejected due to your tiredness. You creep downstairs gathering stray washing on the way and simultaneously put the kettle on, load the washing machine, put out breakfast things, smell the milk and let the cat out.

You head to the loo – the first thing you've done just for yourself and you've been up for 20 minutes. In the loo, you catch sight of a number of things including family photos on the wall reminding you of carefree days spent on beaches and around Christmas trees. You study the faces and each one is a prod of what that child needs from you rather than how much you just love them anyway. Daisy needs a friend round to play, but you're not too keen on her current 'best' friend. Tom looks happy in that photo and he's been so grumpy recently, better ask the teacher if he's OK at school. There's one of your mum, and you feel a pang of guilt that you forgot to call her back yesterday. Finally, your eyes take in a picture of you and Jim on your wedding day, sparkling with happiness. You notice your make-up bag on the shelf, stained and recently ransacked by Daisy, and then turn to look in the mirror – who is that looking back at you? Someone who looks unspeakably tired in a sick-stained sensible nightdress your mother-in law (must remember to post her birthday card) gave you for Christmas. You wonder what has happened to the person you thought you were. Where did she go? That bubbly, attractive and intelligent Kate that could do anything. Ah yes... I know where she went... she went to the land of Motherhood. As you add up all the things you need to do today on behalf of someone else, it occurs to you that some women of your age will be off to the gym, or going on holiday, or off to work doing a job they love. What would it be like to swap places with them for the day? Your mind is racing as you imagine yourself leaving the house polished from top to toe and heading for the station when you're thoughts are interrupted by a cry from upstairs. 'Muuuuummmmmmmmmmm! I can't find my school jumper.' You reach behind you for the loo roll – it's run out! Welcome back to the land of Motherhood.

Being a mother means that everyone wants a piece of you. In the example above the mother, Kate, finds herself thinking about the needs of her husband, her three children, her mum, her mother-in-law, the cat, the house and finally herself and the day has barely started. In the next hour she will probably add to that list by including a wider group of people, such as her boss or colleagues (if she is working), her neighbours, her friends, her children's friends, their teachers, and so on. Notice it says 'add to' which doesn't mean for a second that Kate is not still thinking about her immediate family too. It's an enormous amount of relationships to hold on to and maintain, and it takes up a large amount of time and energy for mothers. It would be easier if she didn't care so much about all these relationships, but she does. In addition, these relationships are often demanding, challenging and not as rewarding as she had hoped they might be. In the previous chapter about values we looked at how values drive our behaviour as a mother, here we can develop that into what drives your family relationships.

Firstly, in the box below, list all the values that come to mind as being important about family relationships. Remember, values are abstract qualities that are important to us such as love, patience, friendship, fun, loyalty etc. (For more ideas to get you thinking, see the list at the start of Chapter 02.)

Values in family relationships...

Looking at the values in the box, pick out your top three that matter to you the most; the three that you can't imagine your relationships being without.

My top three family relationship values

1.

2.

3.

Living out your values in your family drives you every day and when you are not living them, you will be upset, unhappy, tired and stressed. So it's really important to identify your values and respect them, every day.

Assessing your family relationships

To help you assess how your family relationship values are being met have a look at the example below.

Using Kate's values of Love, Loyalty and Fun, this is how she would assess how her immediate family relationships are functioning There is a line called **Me** which is how Kate is ranking her relationship with herself according to her values. It is vital to include this crucial relationship – the one you have with yourself. There is a score system for each value in each relationship on a scale of 0–10 where 10 means that value you place on the relationship is perfect and 0 means it's a disaster.

Kate's example

Relationship	Love	Loyalty	Fun
Me	5	2	2
Jim (husband)	7	8	2
Tom (age eight)	9	9	3
Daisy (age five)	9	9	8
Luke (age two)	9	9	6

Kate can see here that the areas scoring less than six are where she would like to boost that area of the relationship. For example, she really values Fun, but she notices that it scores eight with her daughter and only three with Tom, her son. As a result, she decides to make sure she has one hour every Saturday to do something fun with Tom. Her loyalty value to Jim is very low. She loves him, but sometimes she feels her life would be more straightforward if she just ran the family herself. She realizes she takes him for granted too much. She decides to write out a list of all the things she is grateful to Jim for and keep it where she can see it easily for a week. Finally, her fun score is low with Jim too, so she books a babysitter so they can have an evening out. She tells him they can only talk about the children for the first 15 minutes of their date together.

The relationship she has with herself leaves her feeling low. She finds it so hard to put her needs first when there are so many demands made on her by everyone else. But she also recognizes that she's not the only mum who feels like this as lots of her friends have talked about it. She knows she needs to take action if she is to feel better and more energized. She decides that the value she would like to boost most is loyalty to herself. She will find time this week to nurture herself by booking a haircut and buying the newspaper and reading it.

Now, it's over to you... fill in your grid below using your own top three values. You'll notice that the only relationship filled in for you is the **Me** one, because the relationship you have with yourself has a direct impact on how you relate to everyone else. Remember, this is just your view at this point, it doesn't mean the other person feels the same way about the relationship.

My family relationships and values scores between 0–10			
Relationship	**Value 1**	**Value 2**	**Value 3**
Me			

Like Kate, pay attention next to the scores of six or less. These are the first areas to tackle. List them here, and identify one thing you could do over the next week to move that score up closer to a ten. Make it something positive, practical, realistic, specific and with a date on it, so the first step is to get your diary out!

Relationship to boost	What I will do	When
1.		
2.		
3.		
4.		
5.		

You will feel even better if you take the time to record here the results of taking action with your family relationships. As each one is completed, take a few minutes to complete this table so you are gathering evidence, like pearls of your own wisdom, to refer back to in the future.

Action taken/ Value met	What was good	Do differently next time	Score now
1.			
2.			
3.			
4.			
5.			

This is not just a quick fix for this week. Imagine you had 'spending time together' as a value; so you played a game with your child instead of putting them in front of the TV. This needs to be reviewed regularly and refreshed to check it's in line with your values as you see them. It provides an opportunity to do something positive and proactive about these valuable relationships.

Be free with your laughter, spontaneous with your dance and your children will think of you with a twinkle in their eye.

Judy Ford, *The Language of Parenting*

We saw in Kate's world that there were other key relationships that were affecting her strongly as well as those of her immediate family. If you feel that you would like to apply the same exercise to other key relationships you have, such as the one with your mother or mother-in-law, your siblings, or your friends, then find some paper and carry on – you have nothing to lose and a lot to gain! Feel free to look at any of your key relationships except your partner as we will turn the spotlight on them later in the chapter!

The relationship you have with yourself

Even if you scored the Me section highly on the above exercise, the chances are that you are aware that your own sense of identity has blurred since becoming a mother. For the sake of your family if for no other reason, it is vital that you feel good about yourself and invest time and energy available on *you*. It's actually the best way to spend your time and energy, and the whole of Chapter 06 is devoted to this. It would be amazing if anyone reading this book chose to read that chapter first as mothers are generally much more comfortable putting themselves last. But ignoring yourself comes at a very high price, so be warned!

Involve the whole family

Mothers are like glue, they stick the family together. However, the process of doing that is often so overwhelming that they, and the family, can come unstuck. But, it's not just your responsibility to keep the family happy and in harmony with one another and it's never too soon to create a shared vision for your family.

'Creating a clear shared vision gives a destination and a compass' is how Stephen Covey puts it in his brilliant book *The Seven Habits of Highly Effective Families*. Without this, the family has not had an opportunity to air together what is important to them and how they want to live. All the small, medium and large issues that families face everyday, from whose turn it is to take the rubbish out to full-blown arguments, are handled far better if the family has a vision and some rules they all agree on (more about that in Chapter 09). If you have a baby, then it is just as beneficial to look at this issue with your partner (if you have one) so you know what kind of a family you want your children to grow up in.

To start creating your family vision you need to approach it in a way that's relevant to the age(s) of your child(ren). Read through all the stages of the steps below and decide what is relevant for your family at this stage.

Step 1 – Call a family meeting

Step 2 – Creating a family vision

Step 3 – Take action, live it

Step 4 – Review regularly.

1. Call a family meeting

Why bother?

- If you want to foster respectful communication and negotiation skills in your children and as a family then this is a great forum in which to encourage it.
- A meeting deals with issues in a civilized and helpful framework; it's not just for when you need some crisis management.
- Airing and sharing values is essential. If you don't do this then you're highly likely to create arguments and unhappiness.
- Involving children in decision-making and rule-setting helps them think for themselves and feel their voice counts in the family.
- A regular meeting provides the opportunity to adjust the rules and concerns as children grow and change.
- The meeting is likely to be a positive experience for everyone (if set up and run properly), creating a high regard for having family meetings.

- Family meetings provide an opportunity for positive feedback and encouragement.
- Everyone will want some evidence that these meetings work and that actions from them are carried through.

How to set up a family meeting
Getting started

Introduce the idea over a meal when you are together anyway and choose something positive to talk about, like your next holiday or an outing. Arrange a time for everyone to gather for the meeting assuring them there will be a clear start and finish time. Encourage everyone to come to the meeting with one thing they are pleased about and one thing they want to change. Keep it simple with not too many ideas on the agenda at this stage. Agree the rules of the meeting – here are some ideas:

- One person speaks at a time – you could use a talking stick (one family used the pepperpot) and if you are holding it no one else can talk.
- Listen without judgement.
- No blaming, criticizing or unkind language (e.g. 'You're so lazy you never help').
- There's no such thing as a stupid idea or question.

During the meeting

- Have the agenda written out and appoint someone to take a note of major decisions reached.
- Keep to the point.
- Watch out for younger children getting bored.
- Use humour if at all possible.
- Parents may have the ultimate say sometimes but aim for democracy.
- Getting out of hand? Stop the meeting and explain why and when you are prepared to start again. Don't waste the discourse – use the moment to show what is and isn't acceptable (e.g. interruptions or the belittling of suggestions).
- Remind the family of the alternative to a meeting – could be shouting, arguing, no listening, grumpy parents and children, treats withdrawn etc.!

Ending the meeting

- Once everyone has had a chance to say how they see what's been discussed, encourage everyone to think up solutions.

List them and help to evaluate by saying 'What do you suggest we do?' or 'What would be best here?'

- Agree what will work best, all things considered, and then be certain about any actions needed. For example, a clock that everyone can use so they know they have watched TV for one hour as agreed.
- Congratulate everyone for their participation.

You now have a sound format for a family meeting for just about anything. When you're ready, call a meeting to have an in-depth conversation for creating your family vision. Consider the following exercise to do this. What will it take for your family to make this meeting a success? Where and when? How will you set it up? Who do you need to brief first?

2. Creating a family vision

Using a large sheet of paper draw a heart in the centre and write in the first names of all the people in your family. Then draw seven lines radiating out from the heart.

Place the numbers to the following questions around the prongs off the heart.

1 What is the purpose of our family?
2 What kind of a family do we want to be?
3 What kind of things do we want to do?
4 What kind of feelings do we want in our home?
5 How do we want to treat one another and speak to one another?
6 What things are really important to us?
7 What families inspire us and why?

As you go around the heart for your family, write in beside each prong what the agreed statement is for each question.

Look at Kate and Jim's example answers below to get you thinking.

7. Our friends, the Smiths, seem more relaxed than us because their home is untidy and chaotic.

1. The purpose of our family is to love and support each other.

6. Honesty, fun and loyalty are really important to our family.

Kate, Jim, Daisy and Alex Jones

2. We want to be a happy and adventurous family.

5. We will speak with respect and treat each other as each individual would like to be treated.

3. We want to have time together to have fun and also to experience new things together, like hobbies or travelling abroad.

4. We want to feel at peace and to feel secure at home.

3. Take action, live it

This wonderful collection of words and ideas is your first draft to identify in writing how you want to be as a family. See if you can turn it into a sentence or two that encompasses everything and becomes your family mission statement. Maybe it could be expressed in one word or by a symbol which sums up your family's aims for living together in harmony. A bit like a contemporary coat of arms. However you express this, it now needs to be lived with for a bit, not just left on a piece of paper. It may need adjusting and refining over time, but the aim is to keep it simple and strong and to help your family thrive.

Top tip

It's no good putting up inspirational fridge magnets and hoping someone takes notice. You have to translate the fridge magnets into the daily stuff of family life.

4. Review regularly

You need to make sure you devise a way for everyone to feel their voice counts in the family and that it's not just Mum and Dad who are setting and changing the rules. The simplest way to do this is to set aside a time to review and evaluate how things are going, making sure it's on a regular basis.

You can choose to ignore this idea, or perhaps think it's more like running a company than a family. However, families grow and change over time and if a family meeting is seen as a positive and productive thing to do, it should be something that everyone welcomes. A family *is* a bit like running a company, and mothers are usually the Managing Directors!

What's your parenting style?

By now, anyone reading this book will have different reactions to the ideas here according to what kind of a parent they are. A very strict parent is likely to think that this process of involving the children in meetings and decision-making is giving them too much control. Or they might not be openly strict, but still use shaming and blaming techniques to get the children to change their behaviour or to cooperate. This is known as passive aggression. A softer or even soggy kind of parent would probably not think there was much of a problem anyway and carry on doing everything for everyone. An assertive parent would be somewhere in between the strict and the soggy style of parenting. They understand the need to make some effort here so that everyone in the family can benefit. They will listen to their child's point of view, but not necessarily agree with them.

Recognizing our parenting style is another useful tool to help us cope better with being a parent. Have a look at these examples of parenting styles and see where you think you are now, and where you would like to be.

Style	How I am now	How I want to be
Strict/Cold Controlling, shouts, doesn't listen, uses bullying to get their own way. Children feel unheard and fearful.		
Soft/Soggy Unclear about own needs, lets everything drift, can't be bothered to confront challenging behaviour, sometimes explodes then apologizes. Children only have to keep moaning and they get what they want.		
Manipulative Uses emotional blackmail to get needs met, subtly undermines others so people cooperate out of guilt. Children feel uneasy because the message is mixed.		
Assertive Is firm and clear but warm too, uses direct communication and shouts in an emergency. Children feel secure and listened to, and they know what's expected of them.		

Most parents can be all of these different styles within the course of the day. But it's helpful to recognize your dominating style and what you want to change. One of the key factors in identifying your style is looking at how you communicate and behave when things are difficult and challenging. For example, when your children are really playing up over supper time and complaining about what you have cooked for them (and you have made an effort to produce a healthy meal you know they like), maybe when you are tired after having been up in the night with the baby or after tough day at work. Do you shout at them? Do you moan or plead with them saying how they will make Mummy happy if they eat their supper? Or, do you give up, throw away the supper and give them biscuits an hour later when they say they're hungry?

The assertive style is the one that allows our children to feel secure because they know what the rules are. Being assertive helps us to feel calm and in control of our position in the family when life is challenging. So, with the supper example, the assertive mother would hold her ground and encourage her children to eat up without getting into a battleground. She would remind them calmly that there is no alternative to what she has prepared for them and perhaps ask for suggestions about what could be made for supper the next day.

Features of an assertive parent

How they communicate
An assertive parent:

- speaks clearly and directly
- says how behaviour makes them feel, without shaming or blaming
- sticks to the truth
- uses positive language
- tells the children what they love and appreciate about them
- acknowledges the feelings and ideas of others
- speaks in a quiet, firm voice when their child is challenging them
- knows and expresses their own needs, and finds ways to meet them
- considers and meets the needs of others.

What they do
An assertive parent:

- listens, listens, listens, listens, listens
- hugs, cuddles, kisses and smiles
- has good eye contact
- gets down to the level of the child/ren when speaking to them
- pays attention to what is *not* said
- makes time for others and makes time for themselves
- stays calm when they are challenged
- expects to find the good in people

Looking at these features, which ones are you already doing?

Which ones would you like to do more of and with whom?

Remember this is to inspire you, not make you feel guilty. So, commit to changing unhelpful patterns of behaviour and communication TODAY and notice how much better you feel about yourself as a mother.

Share the family dynamics load

Remember the example of the start of a typical day for Kate, and how she was automatically taking on responsibility for how everyone in the family was getting on, and what their needs were? This is such a common place for mothers to inhabit and it is a huge energy drain. No wonder mothers are often so tired. As well as all the practical things they do, they're carrying around an enormous emotional load too.

My children enjoy time with their childminder because she only needs to focus on them. When I'm with them I'm trying to do a hundred and one other things at the same time, and I'm also really concerned about how they get on with each other. We all have to live together, whereas the childminder's day does not stand or fall if my kids are arguing. She sees it as annoying, but I see it as a deeper and wider issue that affects the dynamics of our family.

Sarah, mother of two boys, six and four years old

Family relationships are a huge concern to mothers, but they need to be shared out so that you are not cracking under the strain of monitoring how everyone is getting on. External factors like those on the list below have a large part to play, but they are rarely caused by just the mother. They are not the sole responsibility of the mother to resolve either.

Here are some key factors that affect family dynamics:

- An upset or change in one area of the family (marriage problems, bereavement, moving, illness, redundancy, exams, new baby etc.) will inevitably have repercussions on everyone else.
- Family conflict is normal. What counts is the ability to make positive changes and not get stuck in unhelpful patterns of behaviour.

- Our culture does not support family relationships – long working hours, relatives being far away, too many hours in front of computers/TV, money problems, housing and the pressure to succeed as a parent.
- Needs change, we all get older, people come and go, and 'upsets' inevitably come our way.

Your partner (if you have one) is another key player in supporting the family dynamics, and he is much more likely to be interested in other family relationships with you when your relationship with him is in a good place. When partners are the last person on our list they feel rejected or even jealous of our relationship with the children. Sometimes your partner may feel like another child we have to deal with!

So, as we near the end of this chapter on family relationships, if you have a partner, then consider the section below carefully.

Remember me? I'm your man!

What was it that first attracted you to your partner?

What do you appreciate about him now as your partner?

Your partner's qualities

1.

2.

3.

4.

5.

His qualities as a father

1.

2.

3.

4.

5.

What are the best things about your relationship?
1.

2.

3.

4.

5.

What would you like to change?
1.

2.

3.

4.

5.

For the list above, put a star beside the things you have control of and that you would like to change. (If there are none, then rewrite the list with things that you want to change that you *do* have control of.)

Time out together

Time out for couples is essential for three reasons:

1 You can focus on each other without the distractions of the house and children.
2 Getting out of the house and doing something enjoyable together will nurture your relationship.
3 Without making time for each other, you drift apart and tension and resentment builds up.

What would have to be in place for you to have some time out with your partner?

- A conversation with him to decide where to go and what to do. (It could be a walk or a quiet drink, it doesn't have to be a weekend in Paris, but if that's possible go for it!)
- An agreed date and time.
- A babysitter.
- It's a good idea to limit the time you spend talking on the date about the children!
- A good frame of mind. Look forward to it!

My husband and I used to sing in a choir before we had kids. We loved sharing a hobby, but that part of our relationship seemed to have been squeezed out as we hardly went out. However, recently, we found out that a choir meets regularly, not too far away, so we took the plunge and booked a babysitter. It's been really good for us to be back in touch with a hobby together. We don't talk about the children either. The babysitter is worth every penny.

Ellie, mother of two children, eight and five years old

Record in the box below what needs to happen for this idea to take off.

Our date night

What kind of date would we like to have?

Is the babysitter booked?

Anything else?

This is not a one-off date. Your relationship deserves this kind of attention on a regular basis. This is to kick start you into getting back in touch with what you love about each other. This will give you both more energy and commitment to the other parts of your lives. One day (and it will come very quickly) the children will have gone and you will be left looking at each other and wondering what to do and what to talk about. If you have been completely devoted to other things during all those years, like the children and working, then the twilight years of your relationship will be much harder. So, the investment is worth it, and deep down you know that. It's up to both of you, not just you, to make your relationship an enjoyable priority.

Learning log

Check you are happy that you have learnt each point below and feel ready to apply it to your life.

- Learn that everyone wants a piece of you and how to manage this.
- Know how to evaluate relationships.
- Adapt to what's happened to you and how you think about yourself.
- Create a family vision.
- Understand what style of mother you are.
- Make time for your partner.

What have I learnt about myself as a mother by reading this chapter?

What is the most significant thing?

part two

two
work or stay
at home?

04

full-time mums

In this chapter you will learn:
- what is a full-time mum
- about life at home with children
- how to keep a healthy perspective on housework
- if it's time to change – thinking about going back to work.

You cannot even simply become a mother anymore. You must choose Motherhood.

Eleanor Holmes Northon

What is a full-time mum?

How do we define a full-time mother? Is it a mother who doesn't have a job of any kind apart from raising her children? Is it a mother who stays at home all day doing housework while her children are at school? Is it a housewife? Is it 'just a mum?' Is it someone who can't do paid work even though she would prefer to?

Many mothers who have some kind of paid work still think of themselves as full-time mothers too, because even when they are at work, they are still a mother. The thoughts and needs of their children are never far away. For the purposes of this chapter, the definition of a full-time mum will be based on a mother who does not have paid employment. She has decided, for whatever reason (and this chapter will be looking at the reasons), not to work and make looking after her children her primary focus every day. She might do some voluntary work, but perhaps this is arranged during the hours when her children are at school so that she doesn't need to employ someone else to look after them. She might have an au pair or other help so she can spread the load or have some much needed 'me' time.

Later in this chapter we will look at what it's like being a full-time mother, the joys and challenges. We will look at housework and how much of your week is spent with your vacuum cleaner rather than with your children or your partner. There will also be a section on developing other things to do (as well as looking after your children) when you feel you are ready to do so. Finally, the chapter will finish with looking at when (or if) it's time to get ready to return to work, full- or part-time. There will be quotes from plenty of full-time mothers along the way who have been happy to pass on their experiences, plus top tips to help anyone who is considering the pros and cons of being a full-time mum.

A growing number of young women who have the freedom to decide have decided that their career can wait, and the delicious early years of their children's lives can't.

Suzanne Fields

Making the decision to be a full-time mum

I wanted to satisfy my personal desire to experience motherhood full-on and to provide my daughter with continuous care.

Jade, mum to eight month old

The joys and the challenges of motherhood, financial needs and career progression make it a complex decision to decide whether to go back to work or stay at home with your child. You will feel differently if you are expecting your first baby or subsequent pregnancies. Before their first baby, many mothers are certain in their mind that they either will or won't be returning to work, but some mothers decide to wait and see how they feel once the baby is born. That choice is not always possible. There is often a financial consideration. Does your income being reduced or stopped mean you have to survive on baked beans, sell the car, give up holidays or move house, or possibly all of the above? For single mothers this is particularly tough as they are even more likely to have little or no choice about returning to paid work. Having your second and subsequent baby(ies) can often see a change in the decision you made first time round. Returning to work might have been easier when you had just one baby, but trying to fit in the needs of two or more children means that many mothers decide to stay at home after baby number two arrives.

Practicalities come into focus too. Who will look after your child? What if your children or their carer are sick, and what about the school holidays? Childcare provision needs careful consideration and there is more on this in Chapter 08. It is also an emotional decision too. Some women just know they don't feel cut out to stay at home with a baby, and the years of being a career girl are **not** going to disappear at the same rate as their expanding waistline. If you did well at school and university and have built up a strong career you will have more to 'give up' than women who have become mothers at a younger age. We are also influenced by what our mothers did. Warm memories of our mothers being at home and having time to care for us inspire many full-time mothers to reproduce this for their own children. But, whatever the reasons for deciding to become a full-time mother, one thing is true, you probably have the rest of your life to work and you will not have the rest of your life to be the primary carer in your child's early years. It's a very tough decision to make and many mothers feel they have no choice and have to go back to work.

Were women meant to do everything? Work and have babies?

Candice Bergen, actress

Here are some other thoughts from full-time mums to pass on to those who are trying to make the decision:

Do what your inner voice is telling you but if you have enough extended family to support you, go back to work at least part-time when the baby is two years old. Work is very important in this society and being economically unviable is a massive issue on lots of different levels.

Claire, three children, 18, 16 and seven years old

Take advantage of your legal rights and wait before making any firm commitment to return. You simply cannot know in advance how you might feel, so hedge your bets.

Jade, baby of eight months

If finances are not a constraint, you should follow your heart. Just make sure that the childcare your children receive is the best whether it's from you, a family member or a professional carer.

Lucy, two children, nine and six years old

What do you need to consider?

This list reflects all kinds of considerations that mothers make when deciding to be a full-time mother. Have a look at it and tick the ones that might or will apply to you.

Area	Might apply	Will apply
Work:		
My career will go on hold		
My job is too stressful		
My job can't be part time		
The hours are unpredictable/too long		
Inconvenient location		

Too much travel		
I don't like my job and I am happy to leave		
Money:		
Loss of income		
Cost of childcare		
Cost of child upkeep		
Maternity pay		
Loss of financial independence		
Feelings:		
Confidence – will I be any good at being a full-time mum?		
Change of identity – who am I if I don't work?		
Expectations of my own, my partner, my mother		
Boredom – not sure I will be interested enough		
Impact on child/children		
Guilt – 'wasting' my education and career		
Spending money on myself without earning it		
Stress		
Excitement at being a full-time mum		
Joy of being a full-time mum		
Fulfilment of being a full-time mum		
Pride		
Focus		
Practicalities:		
Which child it is?		
Juggling everything		
Tiredness		
Childcare		

Looking at your ticks, rewrite below the ones that definitely apply to you under the various headings:

Work:

Money:

Feelings:

Practicalities:

Now, for each area, rank in order of significance what you have written. So, for example, you might decide that unpredictable working hours are the most significant reason why you are choosing to be a full-time mother. Your reasons are unique to you and your situation, but by setting them out here and prioritizing them, you are making a clear record of what needs to be considered in these areas of your life. If you have already decided that you are going to do that, then this is a record of your reasons why. It's possible that this will generate actions for you to do. It could be a conversation with the HR department at work, maybe an honest chat with your partner, or is it time to ditch the guilt and feel good about being a full-time mother? You decide, but if you are going to do anything, then record it here and remember actions need to be clear, positive, specific and with a time and a date – so do you need your diary?

As a result of completing the above exercise I want to...

By when?

Top tips

> Take your time to make any decision about what you want
> to do and don't underestimate how different you might feel
> once the baby is born. Above all, don't worry about what
> anyone else thinks. I spent years feeling second best and
> guilty for not working, but now I think that being a mum is
> the most important job in the world – and I don't care what
> anyone else thinks about me!
>
> Jackie, mum of three, 13, 11 and seven years old
>
> I was 37 when I had my first child. I decided I wanted to
> look after her myself rather than pay for childcare. I had
> been working for nearly 20 years and domesticity was
> enticing and a new experience.
>
> Jenny, mum of three, 12, ten and eight years old

Life as a full-time mum

Congratulations. You're a full-time mother and at this point you will be able to read about the thoughts, feelings and day-to-day practicalities that inhabit the world of full-time motherhood. Maybe some of this will be very familiar to you if you have been a full-time mother for a while. If you are pregnant awaiting the arrival of your first child, you will have a period of time coming soon when you are a full-time mother even if you only take a few days off before going back to work. Whatever point on the path of full-time motherhood you are on, the intention here is to consider what life is like as a full-time mother, so choose what is relevant to you.

Like all jobs, being a full-time mother has its joys and challenges and every mother will feel differently about what they find joyful or challenging. What one mother might adore, another might find unbearable. Some mothers love nothing more than spending time up to their elbows in Playdough and Lego, while others do as little of these activities as they can get away with. Some mothers love every aspect of being a full-time mother, and others feel very frustrated and lonely and would far rather be back at work. Mother and toddler groups can be a lifeline of support and friendship or a nightmare of competitive mothers with 'perfect' children.

Some days you love it all, and sometimes you'll not be able to stand the thought of yet another meal to make or nose to wipe. Overall, the feelings generated by being a full-time mum bring great highs, and also significant lows.

What is valuable about being a full-time mum?

The feeling of being the primary carer for your children can create great satisfaction.

I'm giving my kids a sense of love and security that they could not get in the same way from anyone else. I love feeling that I know them so intimately that I know how to help them if there are problems.

Jackie, three children 13, 11 and seven years old

I value not being forced into a routine based on external childcare limitations. We are free to enjoy our days as we wish. I am there to witness and encourage each small development.

Jade, one child, eight months

I love being there for my children and not having the stress of trying to juggle a job. Generally I feel like life is relaxed and manageable.

Lucy, two children, eight and six years old

> **What would you say you value most about being a full-time mother?**

What are the challenges?

A mother who says there is no downside to being a full-time mother is unusual because it's very common to have times when the challenges can feel overwhelming.

I'd say lack of time, and tiredness are the two big challenges for me.

Jade, one child, eight months

The feeling that I'm not valued and that I've lost self-confidence.

> Lucy, two children, eight and six years old

Although I knew what I was doing second and third time round there were new challenges involved: trying to juggle conflicting needs and sometimes feeling unable to succeed in anything either for myself or the kids, or anyone else!

> Jackie, three children, 13, 11 and seven years old

The domestic dreary laundry, food production, school run and the demands of school coursework and homework can sometimes feel completely overwhelming.

> Claire, three children 18, 16 and seven years old

What do you find most challenging about being a full-time mum?

(Aim to be specific rather than vague, e.g. 'I'm fed up with all the mess' is vague, whereas 'I'm fed up with tidying up toys each day' is specific.)

Dealing with difficulties

A new mother with her first baby is going to have a very different kind of day to a mother with toddlers, twins under ten, or teenagers. It will also vary according to what kind of resources she has. Mothers with more money in the bank will have more choices about what they can do with their time than mothers with limited funds. If a mother has close family nearby, or a strong community network of neighbours and friends, she will have more options about how to spend her day than a mother living in more isolated circumstances. She might be physically isolated or she might live in a big city but still *feel* isolated. If you have been used to working, then life at home with a baby or young children can feel lonely. You need to be in the right frame of mind to push yourself to go and join a toddler club. If you don't make the effort, then you could be waiting an awful long time before someone else thinks to visit you.

Mother and toddler groups are an interesting place to think about. Mothers gathered with other mothers, having a good old moan about their children, their homes, their husbands, their weight (as they eat the chocolate biscuits!) and their other family members. This is positive because as well as getting things off your chest it's often a time for ideas to emerge. Groups of mothers provide a mine of information and hot tips as well as an opportunity to have a good old moan!

Loneliness is a serious concern, and it's understandable that it creates inertia and makes it harder to get out and meet people. If this is a problem for you and you do find it hard to socialize, then how would you feel about using the Internet? You can access thousands of mothers around the world and chat to them, exchange ideas and have some fun. (See the Taking it further section at the back of the book for a range of websites.)

There are mothers who are always on the go, arranging things and filling the diary, and others who are quite content with their children's company and a house to run. Some mothers are very organized at filling up their time, while others drift through the day, with one day blurring into the next and it really making no difference what day of the week it is.

> **Top tip**
>
> Lonely? Lacking confidence? Bored?
>
> Investigate your local mother and toddler group. It could be just up the road, or there are loads of Internet groups where you can share and support each other 24/7 from the comfort of your own home.

Here are some ideas from mothers for taking action and diverting or beating the challenges:

Handing over to her dad periodically. Practising yoga and pilates when she's napping. Long relaxing baths when she's asleep.

Jade, one child, eight months

*Having people to talk to, although it's often hard to admit you're finding it hard to cope, especially when others around you seem to be doing so well. Sometimes it's just a matter of inner strength and faith that it will be okay – believing that things **will** get better.*

Jackie, three children, 13, 11 and seven years old

Little things that the children say and do. Just knowing that I can only do my best and that's enough.

I think supporting my partner in his career may mean redundancy is less likely. We are a team.

Remembering that I would probably be a very 'stressy' working mum, trying to hold on to everything and feeling guilty at not giving enough in either environment! Motherhood has turned me into a calmer, nicer person and if I went back to work I feel that might change! I'm not saying that working mums are not laid back and calm – just that I probably wouldn't be!

Jenny, three children, 12, ten and seven years old

Getting out of the house either with or without the children on a regular basis. I try to have a routine each week that I am prepared to be flexible about if someone is ill or the weather is terrible. Knowing we're all off to the park, meeting friends or having lunch out is better than having no shape to the day.

Natalie, four children, ten, six, four and one years old

Finding your solutions

How does that make you feel about your own challenges as a full-time mother? Do you feel inspired to do something differently to ease the challenges? What about your attitude? Do you see the challenges as insurmountable and just part of the deal of being a full-time mother? If you made some changes, what would your life be like then? Reading about the real mothers, which one(s) do you identify with the most? What is it about what they say that appeals to you?

What would you really like to do about your challenges? Look at what you wrote in your list, and for each challenge, identify three different ways you could overcome it. It could be something you do, or you could choose to make a decision to view the challenge differently and change your attitude to it – or a mixture of the two. Decide what will make this work best and complete the table below – again, you may need your diary handy to make sure these changes **are** going to take place and are not just wishful thinking! Finally, you'll see there is a column to record the impact on you that these changes will have. You might also notice a positive impact on your children and partner, as by taking action why wouldn't everyone benefit?

You have nothing to lose apart from these dreary challenges that are holding you back. Now is your chance to have more of what you want from full-time motherhood and less of what you don't want. Go for it!

My challenge	Three ways to tackle it	When	The impact on me
e.g. Boredom	1. Buy and read newspaper.	Tomorrow	I am taking control and using my brain.
	2. Invite a friend over with her baby.	Ring tonight	
	3. Remind myself this time will go so fast.	Everyday	

Think positively

You have faced the challenges you have about being a full-time mum head on. However, focusing on them much longer is probably not the best use of your precious time that you have carved out for yourself to read this book.

Not every mother can have the choice to stay at home and look after her children. If you do have a choice, real though the problems and pressures are, focus on what you are grateful for every day. When we are grateful and positive, we feel much better about life as it actually *is* instead of what we would wish for, or dislike.

Write below five things you are grateful for as a full-time mother and reread them regularly. Better still, copy them out and put them where you can see them easily. One mother's gratitude list looked like this:

I am grateful for:

- having the choice about being at home to raise my children
- seeing them develop every day
- knowing that this time with them is special
- my own health to be able to care for them
- the support and respect I have from my partner.

What are you grateful for as a full-time mother?

As a full-time mum I am grateful for:

1.

2.

3.

4.

5.

None of us can see into the future and know what will happen to us, so it's really important to focus on the joys of full-time motherhood to help you make the most of every day. As each day passes, it's one less day that you will be spending as a full-time mother and one day closer to the time when you may change your mind, for whatever reasons, and return to work.

There may be another reason that means that full-time motherhood will not always be possible, as this mother Lynn found in her heartbreaking situation.

I have breast cancer and the prognosis is not good, so right now I am doing everything I can to spend time with my children while I'm still around.

The housework question

Exactly what mums do everyday will depend on the kind of mother you are, the ages and stages of your children, and what resources you have. What many mothers who are at home do a lot of is... housework. Even if they are fortunate enough to have a cleaner to do it for them, it's very common for home-based mothers to spend ages tidying up and cleaning just before the cleaner comes. How mad is that?

How much do you care about the housework? If you did absolutely no housework, how bad would it have to get before you couldn't stand it any longer and had to go and get the vacuum cleaner out? The reality of housework is that so often it takes control of us rather than the other way round. We see piles of washing, dishes to deal with, stuff to tidy away, marks on walls, fluff under sofas, dusty surfaces our children write in, windows streaked with finger marks, grimy bathrooms and toilets with unspeakable things in them. Just when we straighten out one area of the house the next one is due for a wash and brush up. It never goes away. The effect this has on mothers varies according to how much you can tolerate before you explode, but it does create a creeping feeling of tension, as there is always *something* that you could be doing.

But, if you think for a moment about the much bigger picture of how you want your children to remember their childhood, how will you feel in the future if your children say that they either knew, or got the impression that the housework came first and you were too busy with it to give them time and attention? Many parents say that housework is one of the biggest factors that gets in the way of them spending time with their children. In Poland, they have a saying, 'a cobweb is the sign of a happy home'. So, what do you really want, more cobwebs and more happiness or less cobwebs and less time spent being a parent and enjoying your children?

Regaining the balance when housework has taken over starts with recognizing how much time is being spent on it and evaluating exactly what you are doing. From today, keep a note of your housework activities over the next week so you can see where the time is going. There is a table for you to complete at the end of this chapter.

People have different ideas about what housework is – what does it mean to you? Here are some ideas to get you thinking:

- Laundry – gathering, sorting, washing, drying, folding, ironing, putting away.
- Dry-cleaning – sorting, taking, collecting, putting away.
- Mending – sewing, repairs, taking for repairs.
- Food – planning, shopping, cooking, serving, clearing away.
- Cleaning – dusting, polishing, vacuuming, sweeping, mopping, scrubbing.
- Tidying – sorting, tidying, redistributing things, bed making.
- Gardening – planning, shopping, planting, weeding, pruning, clearing, tidying, fertilizing.

Many of these things are done every day, and then there are the longer term jobs that are still somewhere in the back of your mind or on a list, such as more major repairs and maintenance, clearing out cupboards, sorting out clothes, shoes, sport and hobby equipment, spring cleaning etc.

So, it's up to you what you record, but the point is to make sure that you end up with a realistic picture of where your time is being spent. Carry on reading this book, but return to the following section when you have got your typical week of housework recorded.

Take charge of the housework

Looking at your housework diary, what did you notice? How much time are you spending on housework and how much time do you *want* to spend on it?

On the following table, write into the days of the week the time you want to spend on housework, and what would be the most important things to do in that time. How much can you ditch or delegate? Are you really the only person who could make a bed?

In the last column, think of one positive thing each day you could do with your children instead of the housework.

For example:

Tuesday, three hours for food shopping, laundry, meals, vacuuming.

You could read a story instead of tidying toys.

	Hours for housework	To do	To do instead of housework
Monday			
Tuesday			
Wednesday			
Thursday			
Friday			
Saturday			
Sunday			

In order for this to succeed, where do you need to put this table so you don't forget to follow it? We have been doing housework for so long that most of the time we don't even notice we're doing it, but our children do.

How else might you or others be in danger of sabotaging this wonderful plan you have made? See what happens by sticking to this plan for a week and record your thoughts in your book, like this mum did.

I just found it so hard to walk past the washing and spend time with my daughter, but it makes me feel so much better when I do. The washing will always be there, my daughter won't be, she's changing and growing up so quickly.

Linda, one child, seven years old

What else can you do as a full-time mum?

One of the challenges facing full-time mothers is losing their identity: losing their confidence in being anything other than a full-time mum. This is particularly true when you wonder if, how and when to go back to work. Boredom is another challenge, so it makes sense to think about what else you can do with your week to nurture that part of you that is really *you* and not you as a mother. In doing so, several benefits can come your way.

- **Confidence** – you can feel your confidence levels rise as you take on a new skill, a hobby, or responsibility.
- **Allaying boredom** – if the world of housekeeping and children does leave you a bit bored, then nurturing the part of you that is outside these areas will help you deal better with the boredom.
- **Spark up your conversation** – keeping hold of or developing something new for you will give you something to talk about apart from the children and the price of teabags.
- **Role model** – your children will notice what you do, and will respect you for showing them you have kept up a little bit of a life for yourself.
- **The CV** – one day, you could find yourself compiling a CV again, maybe with your teenager designing it for you on the computer. You will broaden your appeal by including the hobbies and interests that you have taken up or kept going while raising your family.

Doing volunteer work where I am valued and my brain is needed helps me cope with the challenge of being at home with my children.

Lucy, two children, nine and six years old

What's happened to Me?

Finding time to develop other interests outside the home may sound daunting as mothers are very busy people who don't seem to be sitting around wondering what to do very often. However, opting to make your interests a priority on a regular basis will be good news for you, your kids and your partner. Answer the questions below and see what you discover.

What do I do now apart from looking after the house or the children?

e.g. Occasionally I go out for a drink with some other mums.

What would I like to be doing more of, as the children grow older?

e.g. Volunteering as a reading assistant in the children's school or sitting on the committee of the local community centre.

When I do these things, how will I benefit?

e.g. I will feel I am making a positive contribution to our community, and doing something in my time which will boost my confidence.

When I do these things, how will my children benefit?

e.g. They will see that I have other interests in my life that I combine with motherhood.

When I do these things, how will my partner benefit?

e.g. He will see my confidence rise and I will have something different to talk about.

What could I get involved with?

Here are some examples of the kinds of activities that full-time mothers get involved with. Are they any that appeal to you?

- Volunteer work – school, charities, scouts/brownies/guides, sports teams, art clubs, dance and drama groups.
- Parenting support – Home Start and Sure Start rely on experienced parents to mentor new parents, from as little as one hour a week visiting a new mother.
- Schools – Parents' Association, fundraising, classroom help, school trips, careers experience.
- Mother and toddler groups – organize one, attend them, be on the committee, assist with running them.
- Religious groups – also run parent/child clubs and outings.
- Campaigning – get on your soap box if there is something you feel strongly about.
- Political groups – supporting local and national election campaigns.
- Other – what is going on in your area? How can you find out? The library is often a good place to start.

Make a note of anything in the above list that has interested you. When will you start to reclaim a bit of the old you?

Thinking about going back to work?

It's been wonderful and fascinating to spend lots of time with my children. I also realize that I didn't fully appreciate the long-term implications of returning to work once you've been out for such a long time.

Jenny, three children, 12, ten and eight years old

You might be tempted here to jump ahead to Chapter 05 on working mums. The emphasis on this final part of the chapter is looking at changing your mind and deciding, for whatever reason, that the time has come for you to go back to work. Are you considering returning to your old job, or changing direction to find a new one? For many, you will need to go back to work for financial reasons, and for others it will be because you choose to combine working with motherhood. For both reasons, there will be the following challenges:

Loss of confidence

This word keeps coming back as it's the number one issue all mothers battle with. The thought of feeling confident enough to go back into the workplace after spending time as a full-time mum is enough to put you off doing anything about it. Many women report that their confidence diminishes very quickly, and the more senior the role they had before children the worse this is. Men also experience this when they stop working too, so we're not alone!

Loss of skills

The longer you are out of the workplace the more you will feel that everyone else is overtaking you and your skill base is reducing. You find it hard to place value on the skills you have acquired and polished as a mother running a home, and instead find it easier to believe that your skills are outdated and it will be tough catching up.

Childcare

Mothers find it really hard to justify returning to work when childcare alternatives are expensive, poor quality or unreliable. The rigorous demands of senior positions bring further childcare challenges to mothers expected to work long or unpredictable hours. Many mothers feel more secure if their own family can provide childcare, but in our ever-increasing mobile or ageing population, this is not always possible.

My career was potentially as all-encompassing as my husband's. When trying to take up the responsibilities of a top level job as well as managing a family it is essential that you have family support and help to shore up the inevitable holes that appear.

Claire, three children, 18, 16 and seven years old

Guilt

We will explore this further in Chapter 05 but it is a fact that full-time mothers feel terrible guilt at the prospect of returning to work. They find it hard to see past the guilt of leaving their children with someone else even when it is financially impossible to keep going without returning to work. Guilt is a huge energy drain and is no good to anyone!

Energy levels

Full-time mums often experience the lowest energy levels in their lives so far due to the physical demands and broken sleep that comes with the territory of raising young children. The prospect of trying to be energized enough to take on a full day or week at work *and* pick up the pieces at home feels impossible and exhausting, and for many it is.

Dealing with other people's opinions

As a wife/mother/partner/daughter/friend/sister your identity has been frequently defined in terms of someone else (Ollie's wife, Jake's mum, Susan's daughter, Anna's friend, Jane's sister etc.) and it's easy to lose sight of who you are. Also, these key players in your life can create expectations and give their opinion about you returning to work.

Why do you have to go back to work Mummy? All my friends' mums don't work.

Kath's daughter, nine years old

Overcoming barriers

The interesting thing with these challenges is that they are probably all in your head and not based on much fact. This is largely down to the first one on the list, which is confidence. The good news is that there is a huge amount of support out there to help women returner to work. Many employers acknowledge that working mothers are often extremely efficient, grateful to be working, and well worth employing. In response to this, increasingly, employers are offering different ways of working to make it more practical for mothers to return to work. Work-life balance is an overused phrase, but increasingly employers recognize the importance of working the right amount so that your home life doesn't suffer.

It's important to analyze the barriers to going back to work if you are to have any hope of getting past them. In considering the issues above, which ones do you feel are relevant to you? We know that a lot of this is in our heads, so where is the evidence? Finally, what can you do about it? Try completing the exercise below.

Barrier	Evidence for this	What can I do about it?
e.g. childcare	I don't want anyone else looking after the children.	I can make an effort to ask working mums what they have found works best.

You have considered carefully the barriers about going back to work, and what you can do about them. Next, allow your mind to focus on what the benefits would be if you went back to work.

What would be the greatest benefits for me if I went back to work?

What would be the greatest benefits for my children if I went back to work?

What would be the greatest benefits for my partner if I went back to work?

This process has got you started on the road to returning to work. It could be that you have decided as a result of reading this chapter that the pressures and problems associated with returning to work are too great. For now, you are happy to stay at home. Good for you. The time you have spent reading and working through the exercises in this chapter has not been wasted; you now have a clearer picture of why you are at home and the benefits it brings to you and your children. This will boost your confidence when dealing with the comments you may get about being a full-time mother. Be proud of who you are.

Learning log

Check you are happy that you have learnt each point below and feel ready to apply it to your life.

- Know what a full-time mother is.
- Make the decision to be one.
- Learn about life at home with children.
- Housework – how to maintain a healthy perspective.
- What else could you do?
- Time to change – thinking about going back to work.

What have I learnt about myself as a mother by reading this chapter?

What is the most significant thing?

My current housework diary

Please enter approximately what you do, when you do it and how long you spend on it.

	Morning	Afternoon	Evening	Total hours
Monday				
Tuesday				
Wednesday				
Thursday				
Friday				
Saturday				
Sunday				

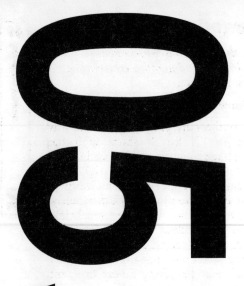

05

working mums

In this chapter you will learn:
- about the practicalities of going back to work
- how to deal with the highs and lows of being a working mum
- how to hit your G (guilt) spot and get rid of it!
- to stop juggling and start thriving as a working mum.

Off to work we go...

I wanted to be able to be that working person again as I loved my work, but also loved my daughter. It was time to put my suit and lipstick back on...

Helena, two daughters, 12 and nine years old

All mothers work, and some mothers are paid to work, and it is those mothers that this chapter is for. It starts with the assumption that you *are* going back to work so what will it take for that to happen? How do you go about finding the right kind of job for you? This is not a career guidance book, but mothers returning to work often change direction and work differently. For example, there are lawyers who are now lunchtime supervisors (they used to be known as dinner ladies). There are doctors who are now teachers. There are chief executives who are now school secretaries – the career path you chose when you left school or university could now be taking a very different route to accommodate the demands of motherhood.

Once you are out working, how will you manage the feelings and practicalities in those early weeks of adjusting to your new role as a working mum? Guilt comes with the territory of being a working mum but instead of tolerating it, how about banishing it and replacing it with other much more positive and productive feelings? Juggling the needs of home and work are part of the job description for working mothers. As the months and years of being a working mum whiz by, you will become an expert juggler.

I once ran an event for 250 people on the same day as my daughter's first sports day. I managed a 50-mile round trip, did face painting for her year group, rustled up a picnic, and cheered her on, before haring back to work to carry on with the running of the event. Neither party knew of the other event, and it all went off okay, but was very nerve-racking!

Melissa, working mum, two children

But, is all that energy you use juggling really serving you and your children? This chapter will give you the opportunity to stop juggling and start thriving as a working mum. Finally, there's the stress to consider. What stress? This chapter will help you identify how you can be the calm and organized working mum you want to be.

How to find a family-friendly job

According to the British charity Fathers Direct, between 1990 and 2000, 49 per cent of British mothers returned to work before their baby's first birthday. Today there are thousands of women out there working who would love to have the ideal family-friendly job.

Whether you are returning to your old job or changing direction, every working mother would love to have a job that gives her the flexibility she wants to accommodate her children's needs and her own. Working mothers find one of the hardest things about working is being able (or not) to be there for the high and lows of their children's lives. If you have a young baby, you can't put a date in your diary anticipating their first smile or step. With school-age children sports days, school meetings, assemblies, drama shows or concerts *can* be diaried. Working mothers feel guilty anyway, let alone when their children ask them why they can't be there or are clearly upset by their parent's absence at these events. Missing any of these moments is painful for working mums, and dads. Similarly, when your child is ill, taking time off work for doctor or dentist appointments or accidents is very stressful if you have an unsympathetic employer. Even when they are parents themselves employers are not always interested in supporting you as a working mother.

> *I know colleagues who have had real problems when trying to juggle work and a sick child. Many parents feel pressured to send their children to school dosed up on pain relief like Calpol when they would rather let them stay off school, but it may not be practically possible. I know mums who have said they are ill themselves in order to stay at home and look after their child.*

> Mandy, two children, five and three years old, works for large charity

Given that you are going to go back to work, in an ideal world, what would be the qualities you would look for in an employer? What will give you confidence that they are family friendly?

Imagine you are sitting with your boss or the HR director and you are guaranteed the job anyway. You cannot be judged on any of the questions you want to ask, so let your imagination run freely. Think about practicalities, think about any rights you might have. Think about flexibility. Think about money and hours. Think about your career prospects now you're a working mum. Think about the company values that you want to see in practice. Look at what this working mum says and then think about *everything* you want to find out from your employer.

> *You will know from before your maternity leave how open and/or family friendly your employer is, so this is a huge factor to consider. Do lots of 'scenario planning' e.g. what would I do if...*
>
> Helena, two children under 12, works five days in own business

Write your questions in the box below, use more paper if necessary!

What I want to ask my employer to make sure this job is family friendly for me.

Think of everything you can!

What do your questions show you about what's important to you as a working mum? These areas need consideration if you are self-employed, working part time or even spending a lot of time doing voluntary work.

If you could only ask one question, which one would it be? Why is that?

Now, you need to make this imaginary list as real as possible. How can you bring in all these valuable points as you set up your real deal for going back to work? Which areas are *you* prepared to be flexible about? Knowing this in advance of job seeking or meeting with your employers will help you be clear about what you want and what is up for negotiation. If at all possible start off with a smaller amount of hours than you think you can handle and then increase them as you need or want to. It's harder for you and your employer to cut your hours back, so start slowly and build up at a pace you can manage if that is an option your employer and your purse can accommodate.

There is a lot more that could be said here about the process of returning to work, and you probably know quite a bit already.

There are many useful websites and books available, as well as employment agencies and workshops where you can find advice and support to find work and be ready for it (see Taking it further). Ask your family and friends how they have gone back to work – do as much research as you can so you can make the best decisions for you and your family.

Back-to-work checklist

Me

Up-to-date CV ☐

Job search – how? (Advertisement, word of mouth, recruitment agency, internet, networking groups, school or local newsletter, other) ☐

Skills update ☐

Interview skills ☐

References ☐

Appearance – clothes, shoes, hair, make-up ☐

Other ☐

Work

Location, hours, journey ☐

Money ☐

Contract ☐

Terms and conditions ☐

Holidays – allowance, any booked? ☐

Other ☐

Home

Childcare (more in Chapter 08) ☐

Diary – fill in as much as possible with school dates, etc. ☐

Chores – who does what? What needs to be done to make running the home easier? ☐

Finances ☐

Pets ☐

Children – what do they need to know about me going back to work? ☐

What other support will I need? ☐

Other ☐

Anything else?

Boost your confidence

Working gives me the confidence that I can contribute something to society.

Caris, foster mum with three children of her own, part-time occupational therapist

If you have been at home for a while raising children, it's easy to lack confidence and feel unsure about your ability to work. You might have been at home for ten years and be aware that the working environment has changed dramatically in that time and your skills are very rusty or no longer needed. Mothers become experts at nappies and nursery rhymes, but how does that fit in around a boardroom table? They worry that their colleagues and employers either won't or don't take them seriously now they have children to think about. Sadly, a working mother's fears about this can be based on past experience. Your appearance may have changed too and the thought of trying to squeeze back into your old business suits is enough to make you flop on the sofa with a packet of biscuits.

Even though you may feel your confidence is on the floor, think for a minute about all skills you *have* been using while you have been at home. Mothers often find themselves having to become 100 per cent more organized than those without children, and organizational skills are highly valued in the workplace. Time management is another one – mothers can pack in an awful lot into one day, especially when their toddler has a nap or when older children are at school.

As soon as my two-year-old has his nap, I can pretty much guarantee a two-hour window and in that time I become an efficiency machine – checking e-mails, making phone calls, doing housework or starting supper – the clock is ticking and I can get an incredible amount done while he's asleep. But now and then, the best thing to do is have a sleep myself.

Natalie, full-time mum with four children under ten

Multitasking is another fantastic skill to take back to work with you. Budget skills, negotiation skills and relationship management have all been polished every day while you have been at home with children.

What skills have you been using that will serve you well in the workplace and ramp up your confidence?

Skills from home that will serve me well at work...

You have so much to offer. There are employment agencies who welcome mothers onto their books as they know that working is important to them and that they are often very efficient workers. Remind yourself that you are going to be a valuable asset to any organization instead of worrying about what others might think of you, or anything else that could dent your precious confidence. Get your thoughts out of your head and onto a piece of paper, using the following back-to-work checklist to guide you.

Keep this checklist where you can see it and tick off your progress. You are not alone; your family will need to make adjustments too as you will simply not be there as much as you have been. When you are at home, your energy levels will be lower – you've been working and commuting which will mean there is less of you left to give to your family's needs. Your partner, your children, your extended family and friends may feel resentful and managing your response to their feelings, as well as your own, is crucial in order for you all to thrive and not just survive this transition.

Dealing with your feelings

The emotional aspect of leaving a baby in nursery when you go back to work is terrible; it goes against your instincts as a new mum. Not only are you torn, but society also tells you that you should be torn, with a variety of messages in the media that conflict about whether working is better for you and your baby or not.

Melissa, works 25 hours a week, two children under five years old

Many mothers feel like Melissa when they leave their baby and go back to work. Be realistic about your expectations and gentle with your emotions. Having had a child, you inhabit a different world to the one that people live in who don't have children. The bond you have between you and your children is impossible to sever, and it's not surprising that you will feel all kinds of strong emotions as you adjust to working. Here are typical feelings that working mothers often experience in the early weeks of returning to work (some of these feelings may stay around for a long time).

Negative feelings

Guilty
Nervous
Worried
Overwhelmed
Out of date
Lacking skills
Unhappy
Uninterested
Unattractive
Tired
Bewildered
Unsure
Stressed
Lacking confidence

Positive feelings

Excited
Glamorous
Independent
Positive
Happy
Energized
Confident
Creative
Sexy
Free
Powerful
Balanced
Capable
Needed

My feelings about being a working mother

Negative feelings:

Positive feelings:

Hit the G spot

There probably isn't a reader of this book who hasn't put the 'Guilt' feeling in their box. It is the feeling that working mothers struggle most with, closely followed by a mixture of stress and tiredness. However, the positive feelings are very much in evidence too, and these deserve to be celebrated and focused on so that we feel more of them, not less.

Guilt and stress, according to Lorraine Thomas in her book *The Seven Day Parent Coach*, have a worrying effect on our energy levels. They reduce it by half, so it follows that if we can deal with the guilt and stress we will double our energy, which is great news for working mothers.

> *I have constant guilt. Guilt at work for rushing out of the office door in the evening and not socializing as much as I would like with my friends and colleagues. Guilt at home for rushing out of the door in the morning and maybe forgetting one of the 101 things that a mother needs to remember to keep everyone happy, in the right place at the right time, and with all the right things!*
>
> Jo, three sons under 16, works three days a week

How much time do you think you spend feeling guilty about being a working mother? The media doesn't help. Almost every week a new study is published implying that working mums are the reason why their children are failing at school, their husband has left them or their elderly parent has gone into a care home (or all three!). Yes, guilt goes with the territory, but is it time to give your G spot the boot and reclaim some much-needed energy for you and your children? You're probably doing your best to combine motherhood and working and there is no point in striving for perfection – it just doesn't exist. However, many mothers say that by working they fulfil a very important part of themselves by having a separate identity outside the home. Older mothers in particular have spent years at home developing their working skills and experience, and being at work brings out these skills, and creates the opportunities for further development. Consider, too, what you are demonstrating to your children about combining work and motherhood. Do you want your daughter to grow up being aware of your guilt, or the fact that it is possible to work and raise a family? Do you want your son to grow up and choose his future partner, and then support her to be a working mother because he knows it can be done as his own mum made such a good job of it?

Benefits of being a working mum

So many parents have no choice about whether they work or not, so if staying at home is not an option, and you have to work, then stop wasting time feeling guilty and focus instead on the benefits of being a working parent. To get you thinking, see what these mothers say are the benefits for them.

I love having a completely different identity within the business environment where I am valued for my skills and experience.

Jo, three sons under 16, works three days a week

I really believe that working you are giving your children a role model to say 'you can make your own choices'. Sometimes it's really hard to do it all, but so worth it.

Melissa, two children under five, works four days a week

I value being challenged, involved in exciting projects, developing my own skills and interests.

Karen, works full time, one child aged two and a half

I like having a separate life where I connect with other people who haven't a clue whether I have children or not as it has no bearing on whether I do a good job or not. It helps me feel better about myself and be a better person at home as a result.

Helena, two children under 12, works full time

Having read what these mothers (who have a range of jobs, hours of working and ages of children) have to say about the benefits of being a working mum, consider what aspects of being a working mother *you* value.

What I value about being a working mother...

When you are with your children, does it really benefit them or you to let the guilt about having to go to work creep in? Instead, focus on making the most of the time you *do* have together and building in easy, simple things to enjoy together. Cuddle them, laugh with them, cook with them, eat with them, play with them, have a big bubble bath and tell them what you love about them. Equally, tell them what you enjoy about your job, not how tired and stressed you are. There are hundreds of things that you do every week which show you are a loving and caring parent, and some of these come from being a working one.

What do you enjoy about being parent?
(It could be something simple, like reading to your children or making them a favourite meal.)

What aspects about being a working parent are a benefit to your children?
(Not including earning money.)

It's up to you to continue to kick the G spot! Regularly remind yourself what you do well as a parent, and what advantages working brings to your family. The money is likely to be essential, but you will find it more helpful to think about what the other advantages are as well, such as being a role model or feeling that you are developing your skills, apart from motherhood.

I feel guilty sometimes because I'm leaving him – even though he has a wonderful childminder with whom he has a fantastic time. I know that I'm doing the best I can for my boy and it isn't forever.

Anna, full-time teacher, one son, eight months old

Stop juggling, start living!

It's amazing how there are 168 hours in the week, if we work three days a week then that's about 15 per cent of our time that we are at work. However, our stress levels can make us feel that we are working 90 per cent of the time! The reason for this is that we can fall into the trap of being unclear about when we are working and when we are not. Work will expand to fill the time available, so in order to cut down on our stress levels, we need to have clear boundaries around our working time. Easier said than done? No, not really. Even if we have a Blackberry allowing us to access e-mails and phone calls 24 hours a day, seven days a week, it is still us who decide whether to switch them on or not. As recently as ten years ago, many working mothers did not have e-mail at home, or mobile phones, and yet today we can be accessed constantly, and it's not always supportive to being a working parent.

Often, in management positions, even working part time, you are expected to be on hand to take calls and answer e-mails etc. outside your working hours. This is seen as the 'privilege' of working part time and the sacrifice you should be prepared to make, even though you are only paid for part time hours.

Melissa, works four days, two children under five years old

How does your working life impact on your home life? How many work-related tasks are you carrying out at home? This list comes from examples of working parents – how many apply to you once a week or more. None of these things are necessarily wrong, but it's important to assess just how much you are working in your own time when your children are around. Even when they're in bed, many working mothers use the evenings to catch up on work when they would probably benefit more from having some time for themselves and their partner. If your work is based at home, then this list applies too, even if your home 'office' is a laptop on the kitchen table.

Work related tasks I do at home when my children are around

- Make and receive phone calls
- Read and write e-mails
- Write lists
- Go through my work bag
- Read work material
- Arrange meetings/appointments
- Think about work
- Worry about work
- Re-arrange my hours or days off.
- Write up reports/notes, etc.

Now, write in your own here:

What is the impact on our children when work creeps in at home? Have you ever heard a child say 'I love it when mummy is on the phone? I know she needs peace and quiet, so I go in another room and play quietly with my brothers and sisters.'

Of the list above, which are the top three areas that distract you from focusing on your children? The trap we fall into is believing that we have no choice about how much we are letting work creep in at home. But is that *really* true? Even if you have a very senior position or you have the kind of boss who expects you to be available 24 hours a day, seven days a week, what would happen if you weren't? Would you be fired? And, if you were, then what would you do? If you *know* that your working life is spilling over into your valuable time with your children, what would you like to do about that?

Most evenings I would arrive home from work with only about an hour left of the children's day. During that hour, my Blackberry was constantly bleeping, and the children hated me answering it. My stress levels were off the planet and I felt really guilty putting on yet another video for the children so I could whiz off a quick e-mail. Something had to change, so I decided to switch off my Blackberry when I got home, and not look at it again until the children were all asleep. It made such a difference to them and to me. I assured my boss that I would check for messages before being at work in the morning, and he said 'good for you' which is not what I was expecting!

Helen, senior partner in firm, three children under ten years old

Make a change

Looking at your list of how work is creeping in at home, decide now to do something about the top three things that have the most destructive impact at home. The ones that, if you made some changes, would bring about more smiles on your children's faces, more on yours and more time to enjoy your family feeling calm, patient and relaxed.

My top three	What I will do differently
1.	
2.	
3.	

Commit to doing these new actions from the next day you are at work and the whole family will reap the benefits.

How to thrive at work

Part of the pressure of endlessly juggling work and home is feeling like you are usually in the wrong place. When you are at work, knowing what you could or should be doing with your children hits the G (guilt) spot again. As you watch the clock count down the last half hour of your working day, you go into a panic of all the things you haven't finished, and if you don't leave on the dot of 5.00 p.m., who will take over the childcare? And while we're on the subject, working mums waste many minutes at work fretting about their childcare arrangements and worrying about who is looking after their children. If that is true for you, then, for the time being, ask yourself if you have done everything you possibly can to provide the best childcare you can afford for your children. It's such a big issue for working parents, that half of Chapter 08 is devoted to childcare.

Having to walk past your colleagues who are still busily working away as you head out of the office to collect your children is not a great moment either. Many working mothers feel like this and if you do, take a step back and consider how are these thoughts and feelings are of any benefit to you, your employer or your children?

Whatever reasons you have for working, you owe it to yourself to focus on being the best you can at work until it is time to leave to return home to your children. By spending time and energy feeling stressed, unfocused and guilty, everyone is losing out. What is it for you that causes you to feel stressed or unfocused at work? What are the practical pressures and the difficult feelings? List yours below.

My work pressures

Practical issues:

e.g. I panic if I have to attend a meeting scheduled too close to the end of the day

Difficult feelings:

e.g. I feel my boss doesn't take me seriously now I have a child

Take action

Earlier in the chapter there were quotes from working mothers about the benefits of being a working parent, and you have created your own benefits list too. Expanding that idea further, what are the practical things you could do to set your mind at rest and stop feeling like you are in the wrong place? It is vital that you believe you can make a difference here otherwise you will stay as you are.

Here are some ideas that working mothers have found which help them to rise to the challenge of being at work.

Try to build as effective a support network as you can amongst friends, family and childcare and do not pull your son's spelling test out from your briefcase during an important meeting!

Jo, three sons

Having a flexible and extensive network of home help and a supportive home-based husband who can pick up what I drop!

Jane, four children under ten years old

Task lists and a diary! For the lists there is a work one and a home one which breaks down into a daily one (with timings) which I usually write out the night before, particularly for a day ahead that has plenty of ink in the diary. I can't keep it all in my head, so this helps hugely. I also print out a weekly spreadsheet on the fridge for the whole family so we can all see where the bottlenecks are. We write in who needs to be where at what time and with what equipment; what visitors are expected; what birthday cards to send; what we're eating that night etc. It then becomes a joint responsibility.

Helena, two daughters

These quotes are to spark up your own ideas to help you focus and thrive at work and at home. Not everyone will have a supportive partner, or feel they can spend another penny on childcare. Instead of dwelling on what you can't do, think of six things within your control that will make a big difference to those work pressures you listed earlier. Fill them in on the table on page 106. Your actions need to be positively expressed and within your control. There is not much point in writing 'I wish my colleague would leave' if that is unlikely to happen. But if you do have a colleague who makes you feel guilty about being a working mother, or having to leave at 5.00 p.m., then how could you view that example differently so it didn't have a negative impact on you?

My work pressure	How I will tackle it	When
1.		
2.		
3.		
4.		
5.		
6.		

Hooray! You are looking at six ways to make a significant difference to your stress levels and negative feelings at work. Imagine what your working life will be like when you transform these ideas into reality. Consider the benefits that this will bring to you and your family.

The happy working mum

This chapter has looked at dealing with the reality of being a working mum by discovering what your pressures are and what you can do to ease them. Most of the happiest mothers interviewed for this book find that working part time is the most satisfactory solution to running a family and working.

If at all possible work part time while the kids are young. Your kids are only young once whereas the mortgage will be there for 25 years!

> Caris, foster mum and mum to three children of her own, part-time occupational therapist

Not everyone will want to or be able to work part time, but this chapter has been written to encourage you to be creative in your approach to combining work and motherhood. It's easy to get stuck in ruts and feel like there isn't an alternative, but you need to believe there is, and that you are capable of bringing about change. Your children are incredibly sensitive to your moods and sense of well-being. You might try to hide your tiredness and stress or lack of passion about your job, but they know you intimately, and they can read you better than their bedtime story!

Doing what feels right for you is bound to have a great pay off for your children. If you are a happy working mother (or a happy full-time mother) then your words and actions will be congruent, that means they match what you are feeling and thinking. Your children, even babies, will feel more secure and relaxed because you are happy. Talk to them about your work. Involve them in age-appropriate ways if you can – once they're in their teens their schools may encourage you to offer work experience or shadowing opportunities. Again, the reality is that our children are watching us all the time, and they will notice that we can make choices and changes that benefit us rather than just tolerating our work and home lives. It's not so much about a work–life balance, but about making the most of who you are, wherever you are.

I have a brain and a uterus – I use both.

Patricia Schroeder, US Congresswoman

Learning log

Check you are happy that you have learnt each point below and feel ready to apply it to your life.

- Going back to work –the practicalities.
- Coping with highs and lows of being a working mum.
- Guilt – hitting your G spot and getting rid of it.
- Stop juggling and start thriving as a working mum.

What have I learnt about myself as a mother by reading this chapter?

What is the most significant thing?

06

taking care
of you

In this chapter you will learn:
- about the roles mothers play, from chef to chauffeur
- how to upgrade your life
- how to control stress
- about creating space for you.

*A mother is a woman with a 25-hour day who can still
find time to play with her family.*

Iris Peck

We are now in the twenty-first century, but mothers throughout history have been experts at raising their children on the basis that if the kids are happy and well fed, the mother is happy too. Her husband or partner is another person with needs, and then there is the extended family as well – oh, and don't forget the family pet. Mothers will, if they're not careful, spend every minute of their day putting everyone else first and neglecting their own needs. They are so good at this that it will take a lot of will power for you to hold your attention in this chapter, as you probably will feel more comfortable skipping over it. Please don't. Please invest some time in yourself by reading this chapter – it will be a significant benefit to you and those you love.

We will examine the reasons why mothers habitually put themselves last. The reality is that being a mother is a very busy and demanding job (Chapter 09 is devoted to what it takes to run a family). There are never enough hours in the day. It's just quicker and easier to keep attending to everyone else rather than carving out time for yourself and if you do, chances are that you will feel guilty about it.

Occasionally I go out to have a drink with some other mums, but we always end up talking about the children and by about 9.30 p.m. we start feeling the need to be home so we can get into bed early enough in case our toddler wakes up in the night, let alone risking a hangover the next day. My husband goes out with his friends and I'm sure they don't talk about the kids or hold off on the booze in case one of the children need them in the night.

June, three children

Mothers are like glue in families so when they come unstuck so does everyone else. But, if you don't take care of yourself, your glue will lose its stickiness anyway. The longer you neglect your own needs and identity, the more likely you are to suffer from tiredness, resentment, irritability, lethargy and temper tantrums. Who wants to live with a mum or a wife or a partner like that?

Even if the only reason you want to work on yourself is for the benefit of your children, then that is better than nothing. By the end of this chapter you will see how important it is for *you* to prioritize looking after yourself, let alone anyone else.

Top tip

On aircraft safety demonstrations parents are told to fit their own oxygen masks before fitting their children's. Why do you think this is?

This chapter will also look at the Who Am I? question. It's common for mothers to feel their identity is now bound up in being a mother, and that they have lost sight of the person they once were. We are in a parenting soup of constantly changing roles from judge to juggler, teacher to entertainer. Some roles are more familiar and comfortable for us, while others leave us feeling under-skilled, bewildered or even resentful. All these different skills we need sometimes feel very alien to us; they are not connected to who we are in our own right. A mother who never wears a watch or falls into bed when she feels like it finds the routines of raising children a steep learning curve compared with the mother who is a born timekeeper. You might be the kind of mother who finds looking after children quite boring, and not really 'you' at all, or perhaps you cherish every minute of it.

One of the ways of reclaiming some of your identity and putting your needs higher up the list is to have a look at all the main areas of your life and work out where you need to focus some time and attention. Where are your biggest areas of stress? Is it at home, at work, or with a key relationship? Is it at certain times of the month, or when your mother-in-law is coming to stay? By the end of this chapter you will have created your own stress-busting techniques helping you to be more of the kind of mother you want to be.

You've read this far? Great. Keep going, you're worth it!

The changing role of motherhood

You are not your mother, and this is not 1965. This moment in history in which you are raising children is moving at a very fast pace and the stakes are high. Families come in all shapes and sizes and many children are growing up in blended families with a range of step- or half-siblings and adults looking after them. In addition, almost half of all mothers now work within the first year of their baby's life, and fathers are no longer necessarily the breadwinners. It could be argued that life was much simpler when we were children and our mothers didn't seem to be half as stressed as we are. How were they able to raise children and maybe even combine work without the kind of frenetic whirlwind going on in their lives that twenty-first century Western mothers deal with every day? This generation have a lot more choices at the flick of a switch, at the press of a button or the click of a mouse. We have more gadgets to save us effort and time than ever before, but do we actually have any more time? There are still only 24 hours in a day, but thanks to modern technology and our own ideals, we can pack in far more than most of our mothers did. We can programme our washing machines to be on in the middle of the night. We can e-mail each other instead of sitting down to write a letter. We use disposable nappies instead of spending hours soaking and scrubbing terry-towelling ones. We can eat a piping hot gourmet meal out of a container within five minutes of arriving home thanks to microwave ovens. The same meal would have taken our mothers all afternoon to prepare. We have more disposable income and opportunities to spend it 24 hours a day if we choose to. But, are we any happier?

We have more food, more clothes, bigger homes, more central heating, more foreign holidays, a shorter working week, nicer work, and above all, better health. Yet we are not happy.

Richard Layard, *Happiness: Lessons from a new Science*

For mothers who experience this sense of unhappiness it is often down to feeling like they are not doing a good enough job as a parent, despite trying very hard every day. They read parenting books, ask for advice and buy every product going to make life better for their children. Other mothers feel the opposite: they resent how much effort is required to be an OK parent let alone a good one, and there doesn't seem to be much appreciation for all that effort you are putting in.

In spite of the internal and external pressures that we feel to be a great parent, our love and commitment to our children (and theirs to us) is likely to be the same irrespective of our moment in history.

And all my mother came into my eyes and gave me up to tears.

William Shakespeare

Your childhood

Thinking about your childhood, how was life different and similar for your mother?

Differences:

Similarities:

Our role as a parent changes as our children grow up. It's common for parents to feel they have just got the hang of one stage of their children's development when everything changes and they feel they are struggling to keep up. In the early years we are mainly nurturing our children and keeping them safe.

I felt that the first few years were largely about making sure the kids didn't die – checking they were still breathing in their cots and stopping them from running into the road or drowning at the swimming pool. Oh, and lots of feeding and nappies. Now they can take care of their basic survival, my role is about guiding and coaching them into the adult world.

Alan, two teenagers and an eight-year-old

The different hats mums wear

As our children grow older we are still a nurturer, but we also become a consultant, coach or a listening ear. We worry about a wider range of issues such as drugs or peer influence – things that are not factors in the early years.

Every day mothers have to employ a wide range of skills. Think about it, you are a cook, nurse, chauffeur, laundry maid, educator, trainer, facilitator, comforter, policewoman, judge, boundary setter, entertainer, hygiene monitor, provider of kisses and cuddles, party planner, homework supervisor, music practice supervisor, pet care supervisor, and so on – the list is endless!

Which roles do you play?

My roles as a mum now:

What other roles will I play when my children are teenagers?
(You may need a bigger piece of paper!)

In Chapter 01 you looked at the job description of being a parent and how that can create a huge pressure on you to get it right. The roles you play can be another pressure. No one ever said that being a parent would be easy, and understanding what you are up against should encourage you to believe that it's fine to be an OK mother, not a perfect one.

Motherhood is the best job in the world. No other career would allow you to be a plumber, drill sergeant, nurse, chef, umpire, banker, telephonist, and international diplomat, and all before 9.30 a.m.

Anon

Who am I?

Ask yourself that question, and what is your answer? Is it 'Well, I'm a mum'. Or, is it 'I'm a secretary/doctor/shop assistant (in other words your job title) and a mum'. Or, is it 'I'm a wife and mother'?

It's very easy to define ourselves in relation to someone else. Look at this list and consider which apply to you.

I am a...

Mother
Stepmother
Wife
Partner
Daughter
Daughter-in-law
Aunt
Sister
Sister-in-law
Stepsister
Foster mother
Godmother
Cousin
Niece
Friend
Neighbour
Employee
Employer
Other

All these relationships have needs and balancing the needs of others with our own is very hard work. Many mothers give up doing what they like doing for themselves once they have partners and children. It's sometimes due to a lack of resources (like time, energy or money) but it's also about having the right kind of attitude to taking your needs seriously. What has happened to the woman you were before you had children? Would you like to reclaim some of her? What kind of things do you like doing, just for you? To help you with this, complete the table opposite. If you are in a rush, make a date with yourself to return to this exercise when you have about 20 minutes to sit down and do it properly. It could bring up feelings of sorrow or resentment, or excitement and enthusiasm so you need to be in a space, mentally and physically, to greet and manage any feelings that come up.

Part A

Things I like doing or did before having children	Often	Sometimes	Rarely	What was it that appealed to me?
e.g. Going to the cinema		✓		Getting lost in a story; escapism
1.				
2.				
3.				
4.				
5.				
6.				
7.				

Part B

Look carefully at what you wrote in the box about what it was that appealed to you about that activity? It might be much harder for you to go to the cinema now because of babysitters, or locality, or cost, but how else can you build into your life that appeal. In the example above, 'getting lost in a story' or 'escapism' could be met by reading or renting out DVDs.

Get your diary, and then complete the grid below so you can bring back those parts of you that have been buried under the motherhood mountain for too long.

What appeals to me?	How else I can meet that need?	My first step will be	By when
e.g. Escapism/ story	Rent a DVD each week	Tell my husband, choose a film	Tonight
1.			
2.			
3.			
4.			
5.			
6.			
7.			

Enjoy filling in your grid and then commit to making it work for you. In doing so you will have identified seven different ways to bring out the parts of you that may be rusty and need love and attention. You are worth it! Don't let guilt or anything else stand in your way. Tell yourself that feeling great when you have 'me time' is what you deserve to feel, and there is absolutely nothing to feel guilty about. Letting guilt creep in will spoil this special time which is for you.

I used to love keeping fit and going to several classes a week before I had kids. I can't justify the gym membership now as I'm not working at the moment, but filling in this grid made me realize the importance of regular physical exercise. I walk the kids to school, so instead of just coming home and eating up their leftover breakfast, I have invested in some trainers which work your leg muscles twice as hard. I could have felt guilty about spending that kind of money on trainers, but I felt great, as they were a lot cheaper than gym membership. So now, three days a week after dropping off the kids, I go for a fast half an hour walk with my youngest before going home. We both love it and my calf muscles are looking fabulous! My husband is much happier listening to me talk about my new levels of energy instead of moaning about my spare tyre tummy.

Janice, three children

This mother has found a way to bring back exercise into her life without having to fit in time to go to the gym. She is doing something achievable and enjoyable, and that is a stretch from what she was doing (or not doing) before. Be creative and flexible about the changes you are going to make – take a small step, today if possible, and reap the benefits immediately.

Upgrade all of your life

Having had a good overhaul of the 'Me' part of your life, what about looking at the other major areas of your life and upgrading everything! Be energized, not overwhelmed, by this idea. It's not about drastic changes but about making small, positive and constructive steps to move your life on in the direction you want to go in. It's a bit like taking the car for an MOT where they check all the major parts of the engine and bodywork to make sure the car is fit for the road. What needs to be fixed to pass the test?

The 'wheel of life' exercise on the next page will help you to work through the key areas of your life and think about what you want to do about them. Life coaches use this exercise to help their clients define which area of their life is working well, and which area(s) need attention. You might have done something similar before, but even if you did it recently, do it again now if you can. You will need about half an hour to complete this exercise but it could be the best half an hour you spend during the entire time it takes you to read this book.

The wheel of life

Have a look at the wheel on the next page to understand how to fill it in, but use your own ideas and scoring.

1 Start at the centre of the wheel marked 'Properties', and list in these six sections the most significant parts of your life. It could be things like family, work, leisure, health, finance, me, personal development, or there could be something specific like relationship with children or marriage. Choose what is right for you, but make sure you include health. If six sections is not enough, you could re-draw the wheel with eight sections.

2 In the next ring out, the one marked 'Final Goal', describe in one sentence what would be total satisfaction in that part of your life. It needs to be something specific and within your control. So, under 'Finance', you might want to put 'to be rich' but that is too vague. What would 'rich' actually mean? Mortgage paid off? No debts? How much money would you want to earn? Or, if you put in 'Family' then what is ultimate satisfaction there? Is it to be happy – a great idea, but how would you *know* you have ultimate happiness? Do you see the difference here between vague ideas and something much more specific?

3 Next, in number terms, imagine that reaching your 'Final Goal' section of your wheel is worth ten out of ten. So what would you say is your current score in each area? For instance, if your final goal in 'Health' is to run a marathon and at the moment you don't even own a pair of trainers, then you would score one or two.

Go round each section of the wheel scoring your area on a scale between 1 and 10. Shade in each section in proportion with the score.

What does this look like? Is the wheel shaded smoothly or very jagged? What surprises you?

4 Next, what would be the first step to take you towards that final goal and close the gap between the number you have now and achieving ten out of ten? Write your first step for each section in 'First Journey Goal'

5 Then look at what will *stop* you taking that step – e.g. 'My children might be ill' or I can feel very lazy sometimes'.

6 Next, write in what you are actually going to do, having considered any influence from barriers – and it's very important to put in a target date so this is a great positive goal within a time frame. You know what this means... get the diary out!

7 Finally, for each area, list all the strengths you have to help you – e.g. determination, family support, money, a car – whatever you can think of that will encourage you.

Have a look at the numbers again – which number needs boosting the most? Which one area would have the most positive effect on you if you did something about it?

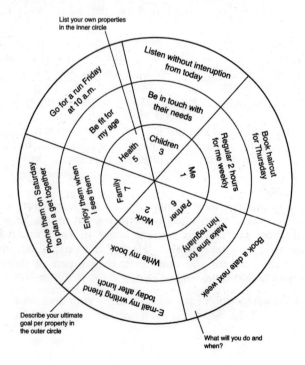

Which area, if you did something about it, would have the most positive effect on your children?

Well done! You have completed a very important exercise to help you see how in balance your life is, and what you want to do to upgrade all the significant parts of your life. Enjoy doing your actions and you'll love the results.

Dealing with stress

The overpowering pressure of some adverse force or influence.

Oxford English Dictionary definition

Being a mother and raising children, running a family and possibly working as well is often a wonderful stress-inducing cocktail. Stress is one of those words we hear mothers say regularly. It means different things to different people. It is influenced by how we're feeling. Sometimes we can have a really difficult day and be able to manage, and other times we can have the same kind of difficulties and feel our stress levels soaring. At this point we go into a default stress position of feeling out of control and the outcome is panicky breathing, snappy communication, negative thoughts and feelings, and saying things we regret later. We meet stress in our homes, in our families, in our workplaces, in our neighbourhood, in our children's schools – in fact, just about everywhere we go and everything we do can bring stress into our lives. It's found in the parts of our lives we care about, because when we don't care, we don't get stressed. For mothers, stress can come in waves according to how we're feeling, who is involved and what time of day it is. If you're aware that your stress levels are spiralling out of control from time to time, then wouldn't it be worth taking a good look at your typical day to see where the 'pressure cooker' moments are that can cause you to explode? This is for your benefit as we are still in the chapter about *you*, but what would it be like for your family if you could do something about the stress levels in your life? Wouldn't everyone benefit?

I'm not superwoman. The reality of my daily life is that I am juggling a lot of balls in the air... and sometimes some of the balls get dropped.

Cherie Blair

Where are you experiencing stress?

Think about the main areas of your life, and consider how stressed you are in each area. Lots of things can influence stress but consider how you are feeling today about each area. There is a 'Me' category, because often we are the creators of our own stress as we have high expectations of ourselves. If we could aim lower, that would instantly reduce our stress levels.

Circle the number you feel applies to your stress levels (10 is highly stressed and 0 is no stress).

Area in my life	Current level of stress this causes me
My children	0 1 2 3 4 5 6 7 8 9 10
My partner	0 1 2 3 4 5 6 7 8 9 10
My home	0 1 2 3 4 5 6 7 8 9 10
My work	0 1 2 3 4 5 6 7 8 9 10
My friends	0 1 2 3 4 5 6 7 8 9 10
My extended family	0 1 2 3 4 5 6 7 8 9 10
My health	0 1 2 3 4 5 6 7 8 9 10
Me (my expectations)	0 1 2 3 4 5 6 7 8 9 10
Other	0 1 2 3 4 5 6 7 8 9 10

What do you notice about your numbers? Any surprises? Rewrite them here in order of what your highest scoring stress numbers are. For example, if your highest score was under 'My home' put that in first place.

Area of my life	Stress score
1.	
2.	
3.	
4.	
5.	
6.	
7.	
8.	
9.	

Take a look at your top three stressful areas – the ones that would really be worth doing something about. If you are scoring more than six, then imagine what your life would be like if you could bring that number down to two or less? What kind of feelings would you have more of? (And, what kind of feelings would you have less of?)

I know I can feel my stress levels rising when there are too many things in the diary. So now, I write in 'blank' time and protect it to help me to say 'No' when I am asked to do non-essential things, like help organize the school fair. I felt guilty at first, but now I realize that reducing my stress is more important.

Working mum Lucy, two children under ten years old

Sometimes stress is caused by events outside our control. We're on our way to collect a child from school and the car breaks down or there is an accident. Or you're just about to go to work and your child is complaining of a headache and then you realize his temperature is over 100 °F. Nothing you have done has created these situations, but the impact on you is significant and your stress levels are increased. It's vital therefore to recognize when you *can* do something about what is creating your stress and when it is outside your control. Having said this, you can still choose how to react to it.

I remember being stuck in a traffic jam and I knew I would be horribly late for picking up my daughter from school. My mobile phone was out of battery and I noticed that my palms were sweating and I could feel my stress levels rising. It suddenly dawned on me that being anxious was making no difference whatsoever to the traffic jam, and was only making me feel worse. I told myself that the school would hold onto my daughter and I could pull over as soon as possible and find a phone. I got to the school and I was the last parent in the playground, and my daughter was quite grumpy, understandably. However, because I was feeling calm and no longer stressed, I had more reserve in my battery to cope better with my daughter's mood and stroppy behaviour.

Jenny, working mum, three children under 16 years old

Your unhelpful stress example

Can you think of a time when you got really stressed, like Jenny was, and you know that being stressed was unhelpful?

As you recall this event, write here what you could have done differently to alleviate your stress? (Leave your family or check in to a spa for the weekend are probably not the most realistic answers!)

Ways to combat stress

Finding ways to combat stress is well worth it for your own sanity, and that of your family. There are plenty of books, websites, workshops and coaches to help you find what works best for you. For mothers, it is essential to find easy and achievable ways to reduce stress – here are some ideas that mums find helpful.

- Go outside for five minutes and breathe deeply
- Leave the room
- Put on some relaxing music
- Light a candle
- Have something you enjoy (and not too unhealthy!) to eat or drink (you might have low blood sugar which is making you more susceptible to stress)
- Phone a friend
- Write anything – just write for five minutes, whatever comes into your mind
- Get some exercise – run round the block
- Stop what you're doing and cuddle a child
- Go to the loo!
- Cry
- Arrange a treat

- Have a rest or a sleep
- Pray or meditate
- Acknowledge why you're stressed (e.g. tired, pre-menstrual, nervous)
- Apologize
- Be thankful instead of resentful
- Change clothing
- Have a bath
- Watch TV or listen to the radio
- Dance.

Write down below what is making you stressed and what you can do about it – get it out of your head and onto a piece of paper. What would help you?

Take your three most stressful areas (you wrote these down on page 120). Write here five ways that you could lower your stress levels. Use the tips above or invent your own.

Area of my life	Five stress busters for me
e.g. My house	Fix the light fitting over the sink
1.	1.
	2.
	3.
	4.
	5.
2.	1.
	2.
	3.
	4.
	5.

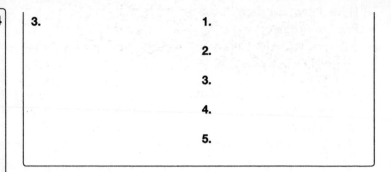

3.

1.

2.

3.

4.

5.

Look at what you have created! You now have 15 ways to reduce stress in the top three most stressful areas of your life. Good for you! This is going to be a big result for you and you deserve it. You have taken control back instead of letting stress control you. Keep it that way.

Be your own best friend

You choose your friends, not your family. The way we treat our friends is often far nicer than those we love and live with. We speak to friends in a way that is polite, kind and interested. We offer help when they need it, and we surprise them with cards, gifts, outings and compliments. We do these things in our families too, but it's done slightly differently with friends. We have thoughts, feelings, words and actions that nurture our friendships because they are valuable to us.

So, for the last part of this chapter about you, please consider for a moment what are the qualities of a good friend. They could be things like kindness, fun, support, honesty, listening, or a simply a mate you have a lot in common with. When you find these qualities in your friend it brings out a side in you that wants to treat this friend well because he or she is special.

How I treat a good friend

What I think about them:

What I do:

What I say:

You are just as important as your best friend, and you deserve to treat yourself to a dose of 'best friend treatment' every day. It might be that you take five minutes to make a nice drink and actually drink it and not leave it half finished. Or, it could be that you give yourself a 20-minute nap before you pick up the children from school. Or, when you have more time, arrange to meet a friend or have your hair cut or blow-dried. Within the word stress, is the word 'rests' so this is your chance to create some rests in your life.

Every day when I have taken the children to school I make myself a decent cup of coffee. I love the smell of it, the ritual of making it and drinking it too. I have my favourite mug just for this moment of 'Me' time.

Lucy, working mum, two children

The stress-busting list can give you some ideas, but it's important that these treats serve no purpose other than taking care of yourself. They are just because you are a very valuable member of society. You are a mother who needs nurturing just as much as you nurture your children. Think of an easy treat you could give yourself every day, every week and every month.

A daily treat for me would be...

A weekly treat for me would be...

A monthly treat for me would be...

And finally... NEVER EVER FEEL GUILTY!

Learning log

Check you are happy that you have learnt each point below and feel ready to apply it to your life.

- Understand the changing role of mothers.
- Know the roles mothers play from chef to chauffeur.
- Know how to upgrade your life.
- Know how to control stress.
- Take action to create space for you.

What have I learnt about myself as a mother by reading this chapter?

What is the most significant thing?

part three

the world of children and families

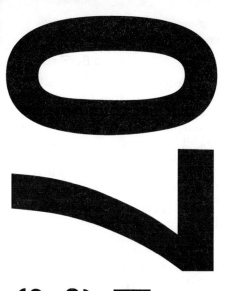

07

behaviour always makes sense

In this chapter you will learn:
- about the influences on children's behaviour
- how to identify what pushes your buttons
- about sibling, friends and other rivalries
- how to deal with divorce, death, redundancy, moving home, bullying.

When my kids become wild and unruly, I use a nice safe playpen. When they're finished, I climb out.

Erma Bombeck

This will be a big and busy chapter to read. It could be a whole book really, as children's behaviour is a large part of what mothers are managing every day of the year. But it's not just the children's behaviour, it's also our behaviour that has a major influence on what's going on in our family. We are just as capable of having a tantrum as our children are, and it's no surprise that they copy our worst traits – have you seen a parent shouting at their children to stop shouting?

This might be a big chapter, and you might feel like you haven't got the energy to read it and do the exercises. However, the cost to you of *not* addressing behavioural challenges will continue to rise as the children grow up – just like your family's food bill. If you put the work in during the first ten years of your child's life they will understand what behaviour is expected of them and what the rules are, and it will be so much easier for you all in the second ten years. A child who understands that 'No' means 'No' when they are five will still know you mean it when they're 15 years old. They may not like it, but they know you mean it because you always have done.

There are four key areas that affect children's behaviour:

1 Communication
2 Self-esteem
3 Feelings
4 Boundaries.

This chapter will guide you through the reasons for this and will help you to spot what's going on when your children are challenging. When you can identify the reason for their behaviour, then you have a much better chance of dealing with it. Aim to be fair, firm if you need to be, and to not lose the plot (which will make things worse). You will have your own style of parenting which could be strict, soft, assertive or soggy, or a bit of everything. Knowing what kind of a parent you are and what presses your buttons will help you deal effectively with your own behaviour.

It's been said that the worst thing we do to our first child is to have the second one, even though we produce a brother or sister mainly for their benefit. Siblings often clash and jealousy in families is rife – again worth a whole book – but this chapter will get you started by highlighting the main areas of conflict between siblings and ideas from other mothers about coping with sibling rivalry.

Finally, bad stuff happens in families. People we love can have accidents, get seriously ill or, worse still, die. Relationships can break down and divide families creating tension, sadness and practical problems for years. Redundancy can also create big waves of uncertainty and anxiety in families, as can moving house. Children can have very negative experiences with their friends and school can be a place of unhappiness. How do parents cope when these difficult life events come by? Do they include the children or overlook them? Either way, they often worry most about what the effect will be on the children when the crisis hits. Even if you get through the first ten years and the worst thing that happens is the hamster dies, at some point something very painful and difficult will happen in your family. As their mother, your children will be looking to you to help them make sense of the dark side of life, painful though that can be. Or, are you the last person they feel they could talk to when bad stuff happens?

> *The Mother is everything – she is our consolation in sorrow, our hope in misery and our strength in weakness. She is the source of love, mercy, sympathy and forgiveness.*

> **Kahlil Gibran**

Four reasons for behaviour

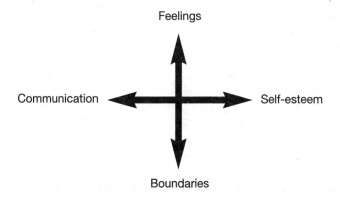

Parents will often say they simply want their children to 'behave' but what does that mean? Are children meant to be able to read our minds and know what we want them to do when we say 'Behave!'? Instead of bellowing out a confusing instruction like that, wouldn't it be more helpful to all concerned to learn how to recognize why they are behaving in a way we want to change? Sometimes it's obvious. As a mother, you get to know your children very well and become experts at reading the signals that are the underlying causes for their behaviour. A child that won't leave the park could be simply too tired and hungry (feelings) and so they shout at you, won't get in their buggy, lie on the ground screaming, or all three. But it might be that the cause of this behaviour is because you didn't warn them it would soon be time to go home (communication) or you may have told them several times, and they know you don't really mean it (boundaries). Or, your confidence may be low, and you're not sure where to muster up the extra energy required to get your child in the buggy and home. Somewhere lurking in the back of your mind is a nagging worry (self-esteem) that if you are having problems gaining cooperation now, how will you cope when they're teenagers?

In this example of the toddler in the park, one or more of the four key elements of behaviour could be in action here, and as a mother, it will be your job to identify which one it is that feels right for you, given the circumstances, which child it is, what kind of a parent you are, and how you are feeling at the time – what a challenge!

The good news is that children will give you plenty of opportunities to build up and use your behaviour management tools. You are not aiming for perfection (we know that doesn't exist), but what would it be like for you to feel more on top of the challenges because you have some trustworthy tools to work with?

Your parenting toolbox

Parenting is not a natural ability all of us are born with. It is a learning process that takes time, patience and the development of skills.

Charles Schaefer

To fill up your toolbox, it helps to first work out what your issues are and how much they affect you. Below are some common examples to get you thinking, and plenty of space for you to use these and to add in your own. The examples show a number indicating how much it affects that mother, and the cross shows how frequently it is happening. Have a look at the table and make a cross in the frequency columns that apply for you. There are four boxes – Communication, Self-esteem, Feelings and Boundaries.

1. Communication

Communication	On a scale of 0–10, how much does it affect you?	How often is it happening?		
		Frequently	Sometimes	Rarely
e.g. Children answering back	8		X	
Not listening to me	9	X		
Shouting	6		X	
Me not listening	9	X		
My own communication issues...				

2. Self-esteem

self-esteem	On a scale of 0–10, how much does it affect you?	How often is it happening?		
		Frequently	Sometimes	Rarely
e.g. Child won't play nicely	7		X	
Child unhappy at school	9	X		
I feel unsure about how to handle challenging behaviour	8		X	
My own or my children's self-esteem issues...				

3. Feelings

Feelings	On a scale of 0–10, how much does it affect you?	How often is it happening?		
		Frequently	Sometimes	Rarely
e.g. Child afraid of dark	9			X
Child often angry	9	X		
I feel exhausted	9	X		
My own or my children's feelings…				

4. Boundaries

Boundaries	On a scale of 0–10, how much does it affect you?	How often is it happening?		
		Frequently	Sometimes	Rarely
e.g. Children disobey me	8		X	
Children not helping in house	5	X		
I am inconsistent	9	X		
My own or my children's boundary issues…				

It's important to look closely at your results and the connection between how much something is affecting you (your number score), and how often it is happening. For example, if you look at the Boundaries box, our sample mum found that her children were often unhelpful in the house, but it didn't really bother her, so she scored it a five. Whereas in the Feelings box, the child is rarely afraid of the dark, but when she is, it is a big problem for her mum (maybe she associates it with her own childhood fear of the dark and harsh parents who didn't take her fears seriously) so she scored it a nine.

What do you notice about your results?

What are the highest scoring areas, the ones that affect you the most?

Why do you think this is?

Pearls of wisdom

Every family is different and it would be impossible to try and solve all behavioural issues in this book. However, there are some pearls of parenting practice which are good to have in your toolbox for each of the four key areas. Look at the following lists. If you feel you are familiar with these concepts, then give them a tick. If not, then give them a star – these are concepts for you to go and find out more about (there are useful places in the resources chapter to help you). Which pearls would be worth trying in your family?

Self-esteem

- Let children take more risks.
- Encourage children to make decisions.
- Encourage children to take more personal responsibility and live with the consequences if it goes wrong.
- Listen to them without taking over and fixing the problem.
- Accept that they make mistakes.
- Let them do more things for themselves.
- Recognizing their needs – physical (tired/hungry) or a feeling (overlap with feelings – see Feelings section).
- Praise them by describing what you see (e.g. 'I love the colour you chose for the sky', rather than 'What a lovely painting').
- Plenty of affection – no strings attached.
- Nurture yourself – read Chapter 06!
- Appreciate yourself as a good enough parent.
- Meet your own needs.

Communication

I love my mother for all those times she said absolutely nothing.

Erma Bombeck

- Describe the behaviour, not the person (e.g. 'Hang up your coat', instead of 'You're so untidy').
- Avoid labels – positive ones like 'artistic', 'cheerful', 'good' as well as negative ones like 'noisy', 'stupid' or 'pest'.
- Small children can be distracted, rather than challenged.
- Use 'I' instead of 'You'. 'I want you to eat your supper' instead of 'You are not eating your supper'.
- Say what you want to happen (not what you don't). 'I want you to stay on the pavement' instead of 'Don't run in the road'.
- Describe what you see so children know what you like. 'I really like it when you help tidy up the toys.'
- Listen, listen, listen! Don't listen and wash up or dry your hair or type an e-mail. Stop what you are doing and listen without interrupting or finishing their sentence or fixing the problem.
- Be aware if you are not in a good frame of mind to listen (e.g. too tired, too distracted) but arrange a time when you can.
- Body language – stay open, relaxed and welcoming. Breathe.
- Challenge without blaming. State the problem, how it makes you feel, and ask their help to resolve it.

There are a lot of pearls here and if you only work on one, go for listening. If you're not sure what to say, say nothing, or 'I need to think about that' so the speaker has a sense that you are taking them seriously. It also gives you the time to think about your response.

Top tip

A teenager came home from school one afternoon. She slammed the door and threw her bag down and stomped out to sit on the back step. Her mother was exasperated and couldn't think what to say or do. She went and sat next to her daughter and said nothing. They sat in silence together for about 20 minutes. Then her daughter got up, and said 'Thanks for listening, Mum, I feel much better'.

Feelings

Well, it doesn't matter how you feel inside you know? It's what shows up on the surface that counts. That's why my mother taught me to take all my bad feelings and push them down past my knees until I was almost walking on them. Then you'll fit in, and you'll be invited to parties and boys will like you and happiness will follow.

Marge Simpson

- Understand that Marge Simpson's advice is NOT helpful.
- Accept your feelings, don't bury them.
- Say how you feel, using 'I'. 'I feel tired/excited/sad.'
- Don't dump your feelings on your children. Care for their feelings as you explain your own.
- Accept children's feelings, however difficult they are, so they feel accepted just as they are.
- Name your children's feelings, 'You seem sad today'.
- Tell people you have a hunch about how they feel, not that you know how they feel.
- Do something you enjoy regularly (see Chapter 06).
- Talk yourself up in clear language.
- Strong feelings block us from being logical and explaining what's wrong – we need to let the feeling out first.
- A cuddle works wonders no matter how old you are.
- Reflect back any 'feeling' words they use.
- Recognize where we feel our feelings in our bodies – are you a gut, heart or head person?
- Express feelings through art, music, dancing, exercise, writing.

Boundaries

- Be clear about the rules.
- Devise rules as a family so everyone agrees on them.
- Say how behaviour makes you feel.
- Acknowledge feelings that demonstrate they do not want to stop what they're doing, but repeat that they must stop.
- Behaviour, good or bad, is how we get our needs met.
- Children would prefer bad attention (i.e. being told off) than being ignored.
- How we are feeling affects how we deal with behaviour.

- Where it happens affects how we deal with it (e.g. it's OK to play football outside, not inside).
- Timing – children raiding the biscuit tin might be OK after school but not five minutes before supper.
- Who it is – it's OK for a toddler to throw mud in the garden but not your ten year old.
- Identify whose problem it is by who is upset. You're upset? It's your problem and your responsibility to ask for help to sort it out. Your child is upset? It's their problem and you can support them by being a good listener. Are you both upset? Go and cool off before you both sort out the problem.
- Importance of consistency – from you, and your partner.
- Agree parenting strategies with your partner.
- Say 'No' softly instead of shouting it.
- Challenge behaviour, don't let it go, but equally pick your battles!

Top tip

The word 'No' carries a lot more meaning when spoken by a parent who also knows when to say 'Yes'.

So, how many pearls are in your toolbox, and how many stars do you want to reach out to and learn about? The simplest way to decide what to go for first is to pick the stars that will deliver the most positive impact on you and your family. Don't be daunted by the amount of stars you have. Parenting is not easy and to do it well you need a mixture of skills, experience, common sense, a lot of love, patience and a sense of humour, over many years!

What kind of a parent are you?

Imagine this. Your two children are watching television and you have asked them several times to switch it off and come and have supper. How are you feeling as you walk back to the sitting room to ask them for the fourth time?

A. Angry
B. Nervous
C. Fed up
D. Relaxed

You go into the room, and no one notices you have come in. Do you:

A. March over to the TV and switch it off and shout at them to go to the kitchen for supper

B. Pop your head round the door and say nervously 'Darlings, um, ahh, er, suppertime...'

C. Stand in the door and say 'How many times do I have to tell you to turn the TV off? You never listen to me, and now you're not watching TV for the rest of the week!'

D. Wander in, flop on the sofa and watch the programme with them – who cares if supper is cold – they'll eat it if they're hungry.

Or, would this not happen in your house because your children only need to be told once and the TV would be turned off and they would come for supper straight away?

What kind of a parent are you? Do you let your children get away with anything, or are you very strict with them, or somewhere in between? What would you say is your dominating parenting style? One way to work this out is to consider what kind of parent you become when you are under pressure, like the mum in the above example who needed her children to come and have supper. Do you shout and make demands, or do you give in? Your children will be used to your style and behave accordingly. If you are a soggy kind of parent who gives in, they will know that they only have to keep moaning and whining or pleading and you will cave in and give them the TV time/more biscuits/latest toy.

Are you a parent whose children know that they only have to keep up the pressure in order to turn your 'No' into a 'Yes'? Or, are the children receiving mixed messages from Mum and Dad? If Mum says 'No' it means 'No', and when Dad says it he means 'Yes', so they work on Dad to get their way? Children notice from a very early age if there is a gap in their parents methods for dealing with behaviour. A clash of parenting styles creates a lot of conflict in families.

Strict parents may get obedience out of their children, but what do their children think of them? Do they respect them, or are they obedient out of fear? Most parents can be a mixture of styles, but the style of parenting that works best for children is a blend of being firm, fair and warm – this is the assertive style.

Being an assertive mum

If you are an assertive mum the messages your children receive are as follows:

- Mum is clear about the rules.
- Mum is warm and kind.
- Mum is fair.
- Mum listens.
- Mum understands how I feel.
- Mum helps me to work out how to solve problems without fixing them.
- Mum explains why she has to say 'No'.
- When mum says 'No' I know she means it.
- Mum apologizes.
- I know what is important to Mum.
- I know I am important to Mum and that she loves me.

This model of parenting helps children feel secure and that they, as well as the parents, have some power and responsibility in the family. How assertive are you as a mother? Which of these features would your children be able to say are true of you? Can you see the connection between your parenting style and how your children behave? When we are soft or soggy, our children won't listen and we are worn down by their behaviour. When we are strict and cold, the life goes out of the family and the adults are permanently in charge, leaving the children feeling withdrawn and fearful. But, when we are assertive, we feel confident about our parenting and our children pick up on that confidence which in turn helps them to thrive.

What's your parenting style?

Our parenting style is connected to the style we received from our parents.

What kind of parenting style did you receive?

How has that influenced the kind of parenting style you have?

In what ways would you like to be more assertive?

Some are kissing mothers and some are scolding mothers, but it is love just the same, and most mothers kiss and scold together.

Pearl S Buck

What pushes your buttons?

In Chapter 02 you looked at what is important to you about being a parent. We can identify our values by knowing what upsets us and creates a strong reaction. What we consider to be misbehaviour is also linked to our values and beliefs as well as our style of parenting.

It's really important to me that the children are polite and say 'Please' and 'Thank you'. When they don't, I get cross because they know they are supposed to. My husband doesn't seem to notice if they forget to say it and it drives me mad.

Laura, two children

Hormones

Being women, we are likely to feel differently according to where we are in our menstrual cycle. Many women say that in the middle of the month they are much more unpleasant to live with. The slightest upset in the family can have them roaring around the house bellowing instructions and not listening, then collapsing on the sofa and crying over a soap powder commercial on the TV. Our hormones may not be on our side, but does that excuse our bad behaviour? If you suffer from premenstrual tension (PMT), would you like to do something about it, or are you just putting up with it? The average age for the onset of the menopause is 47 years old, so you might have a lot of years left to put up with this monthly mayhem, and there are medical, herbal and diet options that could make you (and everyone else in the family) feel a lot better.

What steps could you take to ease your PMT?

Physical and emotional needs

Other factors that influence our buttons being pressed are our physical needs, for example feeling tired, hungry, or dehydrated.

```
What are your physical needs?




```

Think about your emotional needs, like feeling lethargic, impatient, frustrated, fed up, angry, unhappy, dejected, or resentful.

```
What are your emotional needs?




```

Mummy monster?

When you do lose control as a parent, who do you become?

Most of the time I can be reasonable and patient. But when I explode, I become the Incredible Hulk, almost turning green with rage and doubling in size as I roar around the house shouting.

Lucy, two children

I know I'm hopeless at just saying 'No'. My son is very good at going on and on at me until I can't take it any longer and then I start barking orders like a Sergeant Major.

Jane, three children

It's extraordinary how much like my mother I am when I lose my temper. I can hear the same words coming out of my mouth that she used to say to us.

Sarah, two children

It's amazing how common it is for mothers to take on a different persona when they are having a tantrum about their children's behaviour.

Think about the kind of things that set you off. What is going on, how do you react and what is the result?

What happens	What I do	What the children do
e.g. They are running late for school	Shout and nag	Take no notice

If you could pause for a moment and consider your behaviour and the scenarios you have described, what are the reasons for your behaviour? Is it the children or is it you? What would you prefer to do in that situation? Bearing in mind the features of the assertive parent, how could you react in ways that are more beneficial to you and the children?

I realize that most of the children's challenging behaviour is caused by me, not them.

Janice, three children under 17 years old

My behaviour	What is causing this	What I could do differently
e.g. Shouting	Tiredness, fed up that the children don't listen	Get to bed by 10.30 p.m. Talk to the children about school mornings and how we can make them calmer.

Sibling rivalry

*Without a mum the family would always be fighting and
there would never be lunch on time.*

12-year-old

Over three-quarters of British children are growing up with one
or more siblings. The number of step- and half-brothers and
sisters is also rising with the increase in divorce and re-marriage
or new partnerships. Parents find that sibling relationships can
cause a lot of problems, but equally bring joy and team spirit.

How our children get along with one another has a lifelong
effect on them. It influences how they feel and think about
themselves and how they behave from a very early age. Our
siblings are likely to be around for just about all of our life
(unlike our parents), and patterns of how siblings relate to one
another can remain the same over their lifetime. It is connected
to birth order too. A firstborn child can feel intensely jealous of
the second child and that jealousy may never quite go away.
Parents produce more children as companions for each other,
but (as we've seen earlier) it's been said that the worst thing we
do to our first child is to have the next one!

*I just knew Mum and Dad always favoured my little
sister. It wasn't obvious, they tried to give us the same
treatment, but their eyes would light up when she came
into the room, and I just don't think they did that for me.
It's still like that now and we're in our forties.*

June, mother of three children

There is a lot to consider about siblings and, once again, this
subject is worthy of a whole book, or at least a chapter, rather
than a passing glimpse here. The essence of sibling relationships
comes down to three things:

1 How they get on with each other.
2 How parents deal with any difficulties.
3 How we perceive them as individuals and as siblings.

It is also linked to how we got on with our own siblings (and
still do), and how our partner got on with his. If you or your
partner are only children, then your view of the sibling
relationship will be different again. Most only children would
prefer not to be an only child. So, an only child who grows up
and becomes a parent to several children can find their sibling

squabbles quite challenging. They have no memories from their own childhood to help inform them.

I am an only child, and I always wanted a brother or sister. My husband is one of three kids and we have three of our own. When they argue and fight, I feel like saying to them 'Now stop it, you don't know how lucky you are to have each other'. Whereas my husband tells me it's perfectly normal for kids to argue – he says it's no big deal.

Sarah, mother of three children

Think about your own siblings if you have them.

How did you get on with your siblings when you were a child?

How do you get on with them now?

What is still the same about your relationship?

What is different?

How does the relationship you have with your siblings affect the way you deal with your children's sibling relationships?

(Another) Child is born

A birth in a family is a life-changing event. As a child, can you remember your younger brother or sister being born (if you had one)? You might remember how you felt at the time, and that can be helpful if you're preparing your own child or children for a new arrival. How you tell your child a new baby is on the way will be different according to their age and understanding. Your own health during pregnancy could be a factor if you have to rest or go into hospital. Remember, though, that a young child doesn't have the same comprehension of time as an adult. Nine months is a long time to wait. It's important to remain as positive as you can. If you are feeling tired or unwell, then be mindful of how much your child is hearing you say this is down to pregnancy as this could be sewing seeds of resentment about the baby who 'makes mummy tired and sick'.

Introduce the idea that there will be enough love to go around. A child is likely to worry about how that will work. How can Mum and Dad possibly find more love when they have always told me they love me more than anything else? So, it's a big concept for children to get their heads round.

We might know we can love as many children as we have, but for children it can be as hard as it would be for us if our partner got another girlfriend and said 'Don't worry, I still love you just as much.'

Sarah Darton, health visitor and author of *Sibling Rivalry, Sibling Love*

Another way to help prepare your older child is to show them photos and treasures you have kept from when they were born. Tell them about the special times you had together and link it to how much you value them still. Point out the differences now such as them being able to walk and talk and give you a hug. However much you prepare your older child, the most important thing is to make sure they have plenty of love and attention once the baby arrives. Welcome them in at the hospital with a gift from the baby. Visitors can be lovely, but also insensitive to how the older child is feeling. 'Don't you love your new baby sister?' is really hard to keep hearing from well-meaning visitors when you are just hoping Mummy will send her back to the hospital. If your child is suffering from visitor overload (and you are too) what do you think about what this mum did?

The first week we were at home with our second baby, lots of people visited and my older daughter's behaviour just got more and more challenging as everyone was so interested in peering into the cot and saying how lovely the baby was. After a few days, if people wanted to visit, we asked them to come anytime between 8.00 p.m. and 9.00 p.m. when we knew our first child would be asleep. It was so much easier as then it didn't matter how much they cooed over the new baby.

June, three children under 16 years old

Helping the older child to cope

In the early weeks of life at home with a new baby, don't be surprised if your older child does give you some challenging behaviour. Imagine it from their point of view. Life was going fine for them until this baby arrived, and now it's turned upside down. The biggest problem for them is trying to cope with intense feelings of jealousy and rivalry. They can also feel a deep sense of loss for their time with you and these feelings can be bewildering. Your job as their mother is to give those feelings the red carpet treatment. That means that you encourage your child to talk about how they feel even if it is hard for you to hear them say 'I hate the baby'. Strong feelings need to be expressed safely, so explain to your child that it's okay to feel jealous, but not okay to hurt the baby.

Apparently when I was a few weeks old, my mother caught my older brother creeping around my cot with a toy hammer!

Justin, dad to four children

Approaches to take

It's hard for parents to hear their children saying unkind or hateful things about their siblings. It's natural to want them to get on well. Apart from the fact that arguments raise noise and stress levels, it can bring up difficult memories for us about how our siblings treated us. Parents often react in three ways:

1 Denial. 'That's nonsense, you can't possibly hate your brother.'
2 Logic. 'You played together perfectly well before supper.'
3 Advice/Reassurance. 'There's no need to worry, I have enough love for both of you.'

When we get these kind of responses, how does that make us feel? Do we feel reassured, or do we feel unheard and misunderstood?

What are the difficult feelings your children have about their siblings?
(e.g. jealousy, anger)

How do you react to them?

How can you react so your child feels heard and understood?

To help our children with difficult feelings it's important to acknowledge these feelings.

- Listen, listen and listen.
- Use feeling words to see if they have identified what the feeling is.
- Draw pictures of how they may be feeling – this is especially good for younger children.
- Talk about how they can deal with their feelings without hurting the other person.
- Be aware if you need support to have this conversation with your child (if it brings up painful memories for you, for example).
- Remember to take care of yourself so you have energy left to support your child.

Be alert! There's a war on

Green alert

Jamie and Lara are in the car and are bickering about pocket money. This is low-level bickering that goes on regularly, and both of them are trying to engage your attention.

Lara: Mum, Jamie's being mean to me. He's saying I'm a baby.

Jamie: Be quiet Lara, you're an annoying little idiot.

You might be tempted to react to Lara telling tales, and to Jamie being unkind. However, the more the children manage to hook you in to their low-level arguing, the more this will go on. Instead, give them what they want in fantasy terms or remind them of a family rule or value.

'Lara, I expect you wish you were seven too sometimes. Jamie, in our family we don't call each other names.'

If you are at home, remove yourself to a place from which you can't hear this level of bickering (not so easy when you're driving!). The point is, parents find intervening in their children's squabbles exhausting, and it actually often escalates the problem rather than solving it. If you can ignore it, or ask them to sort it out themselves, it's much better for everyone.

Amber alert

Jamie (seven years old) and Lara (five years old) have been playing snakes and ladders. A dispute has developed, and you feel the need to intervene because Lara has shoved the board causing the counters to fly off. Jamie is shouting at her, 'You always spoil the game just because I'm winning!' You feel that any minute Jamie will get really angry and hit his sister. To manage this well it's important to show control, respect and understanding.

1 Acknowledge their feelings on both sides.

'Jamie, you must be annoyed that Lara has pushed the board and jogged the counters. Lara, I guess you are really fed up about losing to have done that.'

2 Appreciate their difficulties.

'It's hard for both of you when this happens. Would you like to stop the game or find a way to sort it out? I'll leave it up to you to decide what to do, and when you have decided come and tell me.' (Leave)

This response also expresses faith in the children to have the ability to sort out their problem. Whatever they decide, you can praise them for their ability to have made the decision, and it hasn't involved a pointless circle of bickering.

Red alert

You have done your best to divert a fight or argument, but things have escalated and you can hear a major row brewing. Someone is getting hurt physically, verbally, emotionally or all three. You feel you must intervene to prevent some serious damage to people or property. When children are being this dreadful to each other, then you will need to go and separate them. Remember, though, that this is not a time for logic and explanations, or for you to shout and scream. This is the time to send in the UN and stop the war, not join the war.

The anger needs to subside and everyone needs to calm down before there is any hope of negotiation. When the negotiation stage does arise, you need to set clear rules about one person speaking at a time to avoid the endless round of interrupting ('He's lying!') as each side states their case about who did what to whom. As the referee, your main job is not to take sides. You probably weren't there to see it all build up and explode, so how can you possibly know what really happened? Deal with what you have in front of you. Two children have hurt each other and need to apologize. They may need the withdrawal of privileges – you decide, and stick to house rules. If you don't have them, then make some! For example, 'No hitting or hurting in this house'. But remember, **never** make empty threats you won't carry out, such as 'If you two are going to fight over the TV then we're getting rid of it.'

The family 'role' trap

Parents have so much power over their children's view of themselves. One of the ways parents do this is to put their children into roles in the family, and this can be done subconsciously. If you have a particularly helpful child, or a musical child, or a sporty child, it's easy to put them in that role and keep them there. The problem is, this creates a pressure for that child, like a label does, and it can produce the corresponding behaviour.

Birth order places pressure too. We make demands of our firstborn child that we don't necessarily make of subsequent children. We are human beings, not perfect parents, and it's normal to find that one of your children is easier to get along with than another. Use this awareness to focus on how you can boost the relationship with the child who you find more of a challenge. Someone in the family might be stuck in the victim role to someone else's bully role. These different roles in families are reinforced by parents, siblings, friends, family and schools. The intention might be positive – we think we are motivating our children if we say, 'I wish you could be helpful like your brother', but this is actually much more likely to create ill-feeling and difficult behaviour. Siblings may take the opposite role, 'If she's neat, I'll be untidy', and these labels become self-fulfilling.

So, how do we avoid the role trap?

1 Treat children as individuals, not in relation to someone else.
2 Step-children have particular issues in managing their relationships, which will require patience and tolerance from you.
3 With multiple births – remember the children are still individuals.
4 Don't compare.
5 When you have time alone with one child, avoid talking about another.
6 Emphasize the effort and persistence a child has made, not the overall result.
7 Value achievements that society doesn't – cooperation, thoughtfulness, consideration and humility rather than competitiveness, materialism, winners and losers.

> **Top tip**
>
> Parents have the power to view their children with fresh eyes and free them from being role bearers.

Having read through the previous few pages, take a moment to reflect on what causes the fights or arguments in your family. It might be something straightforward like being cooped up inside for too long on a rainy afternoon. Think about feelings – is it jealousy or insecurity? What about comparisons or roles? Maybe it's attention seeking, or could it be because you are too tired to handle the situation so it gets worse? Perhaps you are parenting on your own and you are just fed up with having to be the policewoman most of the time. Identifying what might be behind your children's rivalry is the first step to finding more peace and less war.

> **What causes my children to argue and fight?**

What's great about siblings?

Many things. They learn to live with other people and their peculiarities and irritations on a daily basis and that is a great life skill to have. They are there for companionship and love. A sibling is someone to conspire with and mess around with. Someone who understands exactly what you mean when you moan about Mum or Dad. Someone to have a laugh with about something that no one else in the world would find funny.

> **What do you value most about your children's relationship with each other?**

Top tip

Respect a child's individuality. Don't expect the same behaviour, level of responsibility, talents or personality at each age and stage.

Having the support of a sibling can be crucial when the road ahead gets bumpy and the challenges come thick and fast.

When bad things happen in families

It's important to reassure the children that, although Mum and Dad aren't going to be together any more, they still both love the children, and that they won't ever stop being Mummy and Daddy.

Jackie, on separating from her husband when her children were 11 and nine years old

A book about motherhood is like gathering the ingredients together to put into a cake. We have a number of good things in our cake, and we have been stirring it and tasting the mixture. Now it's time to put it in the oven, and it's really hot in there. We might get burnt. When it comes out of the oven, it will be risen and ready to feed us. If we don't put it in the oven, it will be raw, flat and lifeless. At some point in every family, we find ourselves, like the cake, in the middle of a very hot oven. This could be because someone is ill or dying. It may be that a marriage is ending or you find out your partner is having an affair. It could be that a child is being bullied or that a parent has lost their job. Perhaps drugs, alcohol or gambling have taken their grip on the family. Or a teenager is creating havoc and the parents anxiety levels are soaring. What is a mother's role when life events like this arrive in our midst?

Everyone responds differently according to their position in the family, their age and the kind of person they are – you're not all experiencing the same thing.

Belinda, who's husband died suddenly when the children were nine and six years old

Our instinct is to protect our children from harm and to maintain their innocence, but we need to balance that with what will be appropriate for them to know. In chef Nigel Slater's book, *Toast,* about his childhood, he explains how he was not allowed to know that his mother was dying, but because she went to bed a lot, and he heard someone mention the word 'hospital' he thought she was pregnant. When she did die, he was not allowed to go to the funeral. In other cultures around the world, the idea of not allowing a child to be at a funeral would be unheard of.

Listen to their fears and what they have to say. Give them lots of cuddles. Spend as much time with your children as they need. The time invested is never wasted.

Nick, father of two girls who were 11 and nine when their mum died

As our children grow up they absorb how the family deals with difficult and painful events, and that shapes their coping mechanisms for life. If we don't show our children how to cope when bad stuff happens, then eventually they will find something to help them of their own accord and that might be drugs, alcohol, self-harming or gambling. That's probably hard to read when you have young children, but it's part of our job as parents to help children face and deal with difficulty. We need them to build up an inner layer of strength that they can lean on when times are hard. We don't want that strength to be fuelled by mind-altering substances or harmful behaviour. At the same time, it's up to the adults to do their best to ensure the emotional security of the children. The children will be looking for someone to blame for what has happened in the family so they can make sense of it. Help them by being consistent – routines need to stay in place as much as possible.

It is vitally important for children in the midst of a parental break-up to know what the routine is for visiting parents, and the parents mustn't mess with this.

Jackie, two children, 11 and nine years old

Telling the truth

I think that children need to be told the truth about what is going to happen in terms of changed arrangements (that they will go and live in a new house, but be able to come back regularly to visit and stay with their dad), but not the detail of why the marriage broke up.

Jackie, two children, 11 and nine years old

We teach our children from very early on that they must be truthful, and this is what is expected of them at school. The thing about the truth is that however painful it is, when we suppress it the pain doesn't really go away – it just becomes more complicated. Some adults use white lies – a lie that is perceived to be less harmful, so somehow that makes it okay. For example, we might be invited to something we don't want to go to. A white lie would be to invent an excuse for turning down the invitation instead of simply saying that we can't come. When our children hear us say these white lies, what are they learning from us?

We use white lies for a number of reasons: so we don't create pain, to avoid being told off, to make us look good or to get something we want. Think about what your children are hearing and what you want them to learn from you about the importance of telling the truth.

How do you decide to tell the truth or not?

How do you handle your children being untruthful?

When you know your child is lying to you (this is easier to spot when they're younger) it's helpful to stick to the facts and not get into a tangle about the lie. For example, if they say they didn't eat the last chocolate biscuit and they have chocolate round their mouth, state that you can see the chocolate round their mouth and remain calm. Children will find it easier to be truthful if you remain calm.

If you tell the truth you don't have to remember anything.

Mark Twain

Be good enough not perfect

When difficult times hit a family, it's hard enough dealing with your own emotions let alone your children's. Sometimes you feel very out of control and it's natural to feel that you are letting your children down when you can't protect them. Be kind to yourself and don't make it even worse by feeling guilty that you are failing your children in some way. The truth is, crises can happen and you might be able to make them go away, or you might not. There will be times when life is unbearably hard, you are emotionally and physically exhausted, and you are the only one to deal with it.

Sundays were very tough – it's such a traditional family time. I joined a health club with the children so we had something to do, get fit, and have lunch out. Other times, we simply walked the dog, did drawings, played music and watched films.

> Belinda, who's husband died suddenly when the children were nine and six years old

Where you do have a choice is how you react and deal with the difficulty. Our children can tell when we are not being honest and open, so the trick is to 'leak out' enough of the truth at a pace that children can cope with.

Millions of families have gone before us dealing with illness, bereavement, redundancy, bullying etc. and many would say they are a stronger family unit because of what they have survived together. If your family is struggling with a big issue, you are not alone; there are some excellent sources of help and support for you in the Taking it further section.

Don't be too hard on yourself. I came to realize that I was a good enough dad and a good enough husband doing extraordinary things in extremely difficult circumstances.

> Nick, father of two girls who were 11 and nine years old when their mum died

Learning log

Check you are happy that you have learnt each point below and feel ready to apply it to your life.

- Understand the core areas influencing children's behaviour.
- Identify what pushes your buttons.
- Know what kind of a mother you are.
- Know how to deal with your behaviour.
- Acknowledge that siblings can be friends or rivals.
- Have an idea of your resources and reserves when bad stuff happens (divorce, death, redundancy, moving home, bullying).

What have I learnt about myself as a mother by reading this chapter?

What is the most significant thing?

08

choosing childcare and education

In this chapter you will learn:
- about childcare options
- how to build a good relationship with your child carer
- how to settle your child – you know them best
- about finding and preparing for school
- how to get involved with your school
- that you are your child's teacher.

A babysitter is a teenager acting like an adult while the adults are out acting like teenagers.

Anon

One of the hardest things for a mother to do is to trust another person to look after her child. Even the child's father or grandparent is not always the perfect answer to childcare. It's very common for mothers to find it difficult to hand their children over to someone else, and this is even worse if your child is screaming and begging you not to leave them. However, when you *do* find the right person to look after your child, the sense of freedom and relief it brings is wonderful. You can go out for five minutes, five hours or even five days, reassured your child is happy and safe. At some point every mother will be looking for childcare on an occasional, regular, or even emergency basis. Your childcare needs will influence the kind of childcare that will suit you best. You might be returning to work and needing regular childcare, or you may have a special occasion to go to and you need a babysitter. Maybe you're finding it hard work being at home all week with young children, so you want to find another mother to swap children with to give you both some time off.

> *My three-year-old was at nursery every day till noon. Even though I had two and a half hours before I collected her, it wasn't long enough to do much, so I arranged with another mum at the nursery that we would take it in turns to collect our children on Fridays and take both children home for lunch and a play until about 3.00 p.m. That became my favourite day of the week. If I had the children, it meant my daughter had a playmate, and then when my friend had them I could plan in some decent 'Me' time – it was bliss!*

Laura, two children, six and three years old

Your choice of childcare will also be heavily influenced by what's important to you about the experience your child will have under the care of someone else. Do you want someone to be looking after the children in your home or are they better off going to a childminder's home or a nursery? How much does your budget affect your decision? How flexible are the arrangements? This chapter will help you to separate out the difference between feelings and practicalities. Once you have your childcare in place, how do you look after that relationship with your child's carer? This person is being trusted with the care and well-being of your precious child and besides paying them, how else can you nurture that relationship? Whether you have a full-time nanny, a teenage babysitter, a relative, or a full-time nursery place, how you communicate your values and practicalities to your child's carer needs careful thought. Lastly, once you have found the right kind of childcare, what can you learn from other mothers about settling in your child? Some children have no problems at all and cheerfully greet their nanny, or skip happily into nursery, whereas others take weeks to adjust to caring arrangements, and every time you hand them over it's a painful struggle for both of you. Your child is likely to be fine a few minutes after you have left, but guilty feelings can hang around you all day. In Chapter 05 you were encouraged to feel great, not guilty, about being a working mum. Having confidence in your childcare arrangements is crucial for you to be able to ditch the guilt and focus on being at work, or having some well-deserved 'Me' time.

A guide to childcare options

Whoever you are considering for the job of looking after your children, remember to ask for, and take up, references. Most people can deliver a good interview, but their skills (or lack of them) will really come to the fore if they spend some time with your family before you offer them a job. If you can, with nannies, au pairs and mother's helps, ask them to spend half a day with you and the children. Likewise, a good nursery should be able to offer you a few hours trial to see what it's like.

The nanny – live in, live out or share with another family?

A nanny is normally someone (typically a female) who has been trained in childcare and employed by you to look after your children. They might not have had a formal training, but they should have plenty of experience in childcare. Nannies are responsible for feeding, washing, clothing, entertaining and stimulating children. They should provide a safe and loving environment for the child and be expected to plan activities that help the children's learning and development. Nannies are not responsible for general housework or chores, although they should clear up after themselves and the children.

Nannies are the most expensive option as you are buying in someone with childcare skills, training and hopefully experience.

Costs could be shared if their time can be split with another family. They will work full or part time, so if you are working longer hours or you need to travel, then you will need to allow more money for childcare. The cost of nannies often means that they are usually employed by full-time working mothers on higher salaries that can accommodate a nanny's salary too.

Good things about a nanny
- They are generally trained and experienced.
- They can live in and be more a part of the family.
- They might have plenty of local connections to activities for children.
- The right nanny can be a source of comfort and joy to your children as she is employed to look after them in their own home and she has time to get to know them well.
- They might know a lot more about baby and childcare than you do!

Challenges of having a nanny
- They are expensive, and good nannies can expect perks, such as free accommodation, car use, gym membership and paid holidays.
- You will need to make alternative arrangements when the nanny has a holiday or is ill.
- The children can become very attached to their nanny, especially if she lives in.
- You will probably still have to do your own housework, or pay for a cleaner.
- She might want more pay for evening babysitting.
- She might have a clash of values with you about what's acceptable behaviour for the children.
- You will probably have to employ her and sort out nanny tax, sick pay etc.

The au pair

Au pairs differ from nannies in that they have no professional training in childcare and it is not a career choice. As a general rule, au pairs are primarily interested in developing their language and life skills and broadening their cultural experience. Their age range varies from about 18–23 and many will use their gap year before university to be an au pair. It is possible to recruit male au pairs who can be just as good at childcare and housework as females! Au pairs will work for

about five hours a day, five days a week, plus two evenings
babysitting. They will look after the children, and carry out light
housework and errands. In return, they are given their own
room, food and pocket money.

Good things about an au pair

• They are the least expensive form of childcare.
• They can provide an interest for the family with stories about
  their country traditions and even help with modern language
  homework!
• They will do housework *and* childcare.
• They live in so if you are out late you won't have to take the
  babysitter home.

Challenges of having an au pair

• Their English language may be limited – this could have
  implications in an emergency.
• It's hard to interview them in person until they arrive in the
  country.
• They may get homesick or lonely.
• Like any live-in person, you need to be clear about your
  boundaries when they are off duty – can they make food?
  Chat to you? Watch TV with you? Have friends round?
• You have to make time to support them in the early weeks
  while they get to know your family, the area they are living in
  and how to phone home.

Mother's helps

Mother's helps are similar to nannies, but usually without
formal training. They work alongside a mother as well as having
full charge of the home and children. They should have
experience with children or have worked in a nursery, but they
are employed to do what the mother needs, rather than just look
after the children. They can be a good answer for mothers who
also work from home or work part time, and want a
combination of housework and childcare.

Good things about a mother's help

• They are more flexible than a nanny as they will do what you
  need, so they might look after your toddler, do the
  supermarket run and clean the bathroom in the course of the
  day.

- They probably live out – although some might see this as a challenge.
- They are cheaper than a nanny.
- They are more experienced with children than an au pair.

Challenges of having a mother's help
- They might not be properly trained in childcare.
- You are likely to have more contact with them so the job description needs clarity.

Grandparent or other relative

Grandparents or other family members can be a wonderful answer to childcare. They usually don't want to be paid, and they are highly likely to love your children almost as much as you do, and have their best interests at heart. In our increasingly mobile population, fewer families have a relative nearby who can be the childcare provider. Even if they are local, sometimes the last person you would want looking after your children is a relative.

Good things about relatives
- They are usually free.
- They love your children.
- They can develop a close relationship with your children.
- They might behave differently towards your children compared to how they brought you up, e.g. more relaxed and less strict.
- They can be flexible about arrangements.
- They have experience with children.

Challenges of using a relative
- Your parenting styles can clash.
- They can interfere with your values.
- It's not a commercial arrangement so if problems arise it is more complicated to resolve them.
- They might be unreliable and think it doesn't matter.
- If they're elderly, your children could become too much for them to look after.

Friend

Using a friend for childcare can be a great solution, but like using family members, make extra sure you are clear about what you need and what your boundaries are.

Good things about friends

- They might be available for little or no cost, especially if you arrange to swap.
- They may be familiar with the ages and stages of your children (perhaps they have children).
- They may have children for yours to play with.
- They are usually local and willing to be flexible.

Challenges of using a friend

- Again, it might not be a commercial arrangement, so any problems could be awkward to deal with.
- There could be a clash of parenting styles and values.
- They might be unreliable, and not take your needs seriously enough.
- They may not be experienced or trained to deal with childcare emergencies.
- They might be resentful that while they have your children, you have gone off to the gym or to work.

Babysitter

A babysitter is someone who will occasionally look after your children during the day or in the evening. Choosing a babysitter is just as important as choosing any kind of childcare and you have to be just as rigorous in your vetting. They will be left in sole charge of your children and, even if it is only for an hour or so, you have to be sure of their competence. There is currently no law about the age a babysitter needs to be in order to be left in sole charge of children. The National Society for the Prevention of Cruelty to Children (NSPCC) recommends that a babysitter should be at least 16 years old. Anyone under 16 cannot be charged with neglect or ill treatment of children in their care. This means that if you leave your children with someone under 16 you are still responsible for them. If there is an emergency, such as a fire or a child has an accident, you could be charged with neglect.

Good things about babysitters

- They are relatively inexpensive.
- Teenagers can be playful and energetic which can be lovely for your children.
- They might help with homework or music practice for older children.

- They might stay the night instead of you having to take them home.
- It gives you a well-deserved night out.

Challenges of having a babysitter
- Their experience varies.
- They might have little control over your children if they behave badly.
- They might want more money after midnight.
- They might have to be taken home by you or by taxi.
- They eat all your chocolate biscuits, and don't usually wash up or tidy up toys.

Childminder

Registered childminders are professional childcarers who work in their own homes to provide care and learning opportunities for other people's children in a family setting.

Childminders are usually registered to look after up to three children under five years old and three children aged between five and eight years old, including their own children. They may also look after older children up to the age of 14.

All childminders who are registered with Ofsted or Care Standard Inspectorate for Wales have been checked by the Criminal Records Bureau, are insured, have first aid training and have had a health check. As well as induction training, many childminders undertake childcare qualifications or attend workshops on subjects like nutrition, sign language or business management.

Good things about childminders
- They care for your children in a home environment.
- They are usually cheaper than a nanny, and more experienced than an au pair or mother's help.
- They usually have good links with local children's activities, nurseries and schools.
- They can be flexible and offer extended care.

Challenges of having a childminder
- They might be inflexible!
- There could be a clash over parenting styles and values, and you might not be aware of this initially.

- They are using their home, not yours, so add on drop-off and pick-up time.
- You need alternative arrangements if your childminder is ill or on holiday.

Nursery and workplace nursery

There are three types of nurseries:

1 **Council nurseries** – these are free but it can be very difficult to get places. They are usually reserved for children with special circumstances, i.e. lone-parent families, etc.
2 **Private nurseries** – these are fee-paying nurseries and although they are the most expensive option they are springing up everywhere and you are very likely to find an available place in one of them. You can find private nurseries that are prepared to be more flexible over hours. Some have extra services such as Internet access so that you can log on and see your child during the day. Increasingly, they offer organic food at mealtimes or extra music, dance or language lessons.
3 **Nurseries in the workplace** – places in these nurseries are reserved mainly for children of employees, but if there are any extra spaces then non-employees will be considered although they will not be eligible for employee discounts. If you hear of a brilliant workplace nursery in your area, it's definitely worth a visit.

Some nurseries are run according to a particular style of childcare and education such as Montessori, named after Maria Montessori, or the Rudolph Steiner schools. If you are interested in alternative types of nursery care, see the Taking it further section.

Good things about nurseries
- Nurseries are very reliable – they are always open and you are not relying on one individual who may let you down at the last minute.
- Nurseries can give children early confidence and be a great starting block for school as they get children used to being away from their mum and help them learn to operate in an environment with other children.
- A workplace nursery can give a mother peace of mind knowing that her child is being cared for in the same location as her work.

Challenges of using nurseries

- If your child is very shy they may find life in a nursery rather overwhelming and there is not much one-to-one care.
- If your child is sick they won't be accepted into the nursery and you will have to care for them at home. If you decide on a nursery you may need to find family back-up or a babysitter you can call on at the last moment if your child is ill and you cannot take the time off work to look after them.
- Most nurseries cannot be expected to be flexible – you need to be on time to pick up your child.

After-school, breakfast and holiday clubs

An after-school club is a place for children to go after the school day has finished but office hours haven't, usually from around 3.30 p.m. to 6.00 p.m. The club may be in your child's school, another local school or different premises altogether. Fun and relaxing games, sports or art and crafts are provided as well as snacks and drinks for children, and all under the care of trained playworkers.

A breakfast club is a place where children can be dropped off before school and enjoy breakfast together and some activities under the supervision of qualified staff.

A holiday playscheme operates in the school holidays and offers groups of children a range of organized activities, from art and crafts to outings.

Good things about clubs

- An after-school club, breakfast club or playscheme which caters for under-eights for more than two hours a day will be registered and regularly inspected. If it's registered, it will be run by approved playworkers, around half of whom will be trained. It can bridge those awkward gaps between school and work hours.
- Your child will be among a group of other children, some younger, some older, but they will know many of them and it will be a familiar environment.
- Your child will have access to a variety of play opportunities.
- You may be able to opt for a regular place, and the consistency of the arrangement will benefit your child.

Challenges of using clubs

- After-school clubs can be very busy and your child may simply prefer to, or need to, relax at home.
- Find out how much television the staff allow the children to watch.
- Out-of-school care may be a bit overwhelming for a younger or shy child. If your child is attending an after-school club every day, it can be hard for them to have time on their own, meet their friends, or follow their own particular interests.
- The staff won't be able to look after your child if they are ill.

Check the Taking it further section for websites and organizations for lots more help about childcare choices.

What's really important to you about childcare?

> *Often we expect too much from a childcarer. We want them to be like us, smart, bright, witty, responsible, loving, imaginative, patient, well-mannered and cheerful, but not so smart that she's going to be bored after a couple of months and leave us to go to medical school.*

Louise Lague

When you're deciding on the kind of childcare you want and can afford, the first thing to do is to make a list of what are the qualities you want to find in a childcarer or a nursery. You can certainly ask friends and family what they think is important, and do your own research too, but ultimately you will know what is best for your children.

Here are some useful questions to consider when choosing childcare:

1 What are the qualities I want to find in a childcarer (e.g. patience, kindness, creativity etc.)?
2 How do I want my child to spend their day in childcare?
3 What kind of things would I like them to do with my child?
4 What would I want them to do about disciplining my child?
5 How will I cope if there is an emergency and my child or their carer is ill?
6 How do I want a childcarer to treat our home and possessions?
7 How much flexibility do I need?

8 How confident am I at interviewing and taking up references?
9 What is my childcare budget, including holiday and sick pay if needed?
10 What's the one question missing off this list that *you* think would be good to consider?

Remember, parents have wonderful intuition and gut instinct about what is going to work best for them and their children. You might be tempted to feel guilty, but your children have much to gain from being cared for by different people.

Who looks after my child?	What are the benefits to my child?	What are the benefits to me?
e.g. My au pair	Access to a girl from another country.	She often has more energy than I do.

If you're away from your children, it's understandable to feel you're missing out on being with them. Find out from your childcarer or nursery what your children enjoy doing during the time they are there and imagine them doing that.

I have a great nanny, and she keeps a log of what they have done all day, and leaves any messages for me. I read the log when I get home and it gives me a picture of what kind of a day my daughter has had.

Karen, full-time working mum of three-year-old

Do everything you can to keep your confidence up about your childcare. At the same time, if your child is *really* unhappy, and you have either a hunch or evidence that the childcare they have is not working, then have the guts to change it. Every mother wants to leave their children with Mary Poppins, and sometimes you might have to try several different childcare options before your version of Mary Poppins comes your way.

Looking after the carer

You have placed your most precious possession into the care of someone else. You have put in a huge amount of effort to find the best childcare you can afford. Sometimes, after that, many mothers breathe a sigh of relief and rush back to work. However, all relationships, especially the one with your childcarer, will need nurturing. If you neglect her, then don't be surprised if misunderstandings and resentment build up. This could lead to her not caring as much about her job, or just leaving. Here are some top tips from mothers about looking after their childcarers:

- Find out and then remember her birthday.
- Be generous – make a point of coming home early sometimes to either spend some time catching up with her, or letting her go home early.
- Create a good system to communicate with each other. It could be a logbook, e-mail, texting or leaving notes, but it's better to over-communicate than under-communicate.
- Ask for her opinion.
- Listen to her even if you think you don't have the time – actually you don't have the time *not* to listen.
- Have a regular review of her pay and conditions of work.
- If you have to challenge her, instead of yelling accusations, speak to her respectfully and stick to the facts. Ask for her help to identify solutions.
- Show an interest in her life outside of her job with you. Get to know her own family.
- Never take her for granted or assume she is working for you until your children leave home. She might appear to love her job and your children, but one day she could have very sound reasons for leaving and you will have to live with that *and* have just a few weeks to replace her.

I asked our nanny at her interview if she would mind if I rang her mother. It gave me a good insight into the kind of family she had come from, and it meant if there was an emergency, I could contact her family immediately.

Sarah, two children under eight

Settling your child

Helping your child to settle in with new childcare is largely down to their age and your attitude. A three-month-old baby is going to be a different prospect to a two year old or an eight year old. It will be different for them if they are being cared for in their own home, or away from home with a childminder, nursery or after-school club. You will feel differently if this is your first child or your last child. However, your own state will be a big clue to your children, even a baby, if this childcare idea is welcome or not. If you are anxious and fretful, what is the message you are sending your children? If you are relaxed and positive about how much fun they're going to have with this great new nanny then that will have a positive impact on your children's feelings. It's natural for children to be a bit clingy – they love you after all, not the nursery or the nanny, yet. Here are some ideas for settling children – make a note of the ones that appeal to you.

Preparation

I forgot to tell my three-year-old that he would need to change his shoes to go outside playtime at nursery and he was very upset about this, especially since I had also forgotten to send in a pair of Wellies. Whoops!

Laura, two children

Preparation is key! Spend time explaining to your children what the childcare arrangements will be so they have a clear idea about what will be happening and when.

Go back to work gradually

If you can afford it, see if your employer will let you start back to work part time for the first couple of weeks. This gives you and your child more time to adjust. Alternatively, try leaving your child with the carer for a few sessions before you return to work.

Affection

A big kiss and cuddle, followed by a clear 'Bye, bye, see you later' are essential. If they are old enough, be specific about your return time, e.g. 'I'll be back after story time'. By clearly indicating that you're leaving, your child comes to understand that there's a pattern to the day, and that you do come back when you say you will. It's tempting to sneak away when your toddler is not looking, but in the long run this is likely to make them less able to trust you and feel unsettled for longer. Explain to them that you will be thinking about them during the day, and show them a favourite photo of them that you have on your desk at work or in your handbag.

Use your time wisely

Be prepared to spend time helping them to settle. There is nothing more upsetting than having to leave a child screaming while you rush off to work. Ask your nursery or childminder what they recommend. If your child is crying, find out how quickly they settled down once you had gone.

Be really pleased to see them when you come home (or pick them up) and be polite and thankful to the childminder too.

Leaving work was a bit of a headache as I was rushing to get to the childminder and if the traffic was bad then by the time I arrived I was anxious and exhausted. To make matters worse, my five-year-old was sometimes really grumpy and rude to me. I decided to leave work five minutes early, and phone my son on the way and have a chat. It meant he was back in touch with me before I arrived – much better.

Sarah, two children

Catch up of the day's events

Encourage them to tell you about their day and you can tell them about yours. You have been apart from someone you love very much and it's only natural to want to find out what they have been doing. It's OK to say you missed them, but don't over do it. Instead, talk about what you imagined them doing such as painting, or playing in the park. Don't be surprised if they're not very interested in speaking to you when you meet up again. Sometimes they are really tired and just don't feel like talking about their day yet – that is true whatever age we are!

Children might give you a hard time when you re-engage with them. They thrive on routine and the changeover time can be unsettling for them so they can be hurtful and unkind, which is not what you want when you have been looking forward to seeing them. Remember though, you are the adult, so within reason aim to ignore their bad behaviour. If they are unacceptably rude to you, explain that you have been looking forward to seeing them and when they're ready to speak nicely to you, you are ready to listen.

I once heard about a very busy, wealthy lady who would come home loaded down with shopping bags. When she came in, she just dropped the bags and sat on the floor in the hallway and let her children climb all over her. They were excited and she made a conscious decision to welcome their need to make contact with her. After a few minutes, they had had their fill of her, and she was left in peace to unpack her bags and reconnect with the rest of her domestic world.

Anon

Time for school

The first time you leave your child at school you're faced with a tough decision – down the pub or back to bed.

Jo Brand

At what point does it occur to you to think about schooling for your child? As you watch your pregnancy test stick turn blue or when you receive a letter from the council asking you to choose a school for your four year old? Most of us will be somewhere in between these two points. In the UK, children will start school during the academic year in which they turn five, unless you decide to educate them from home. (If you do that, then you still have to satisfy your local education authority that you are educating your child from five.) Who wouldn't love a great local school, but that's not so easy to find, and if you do, plenty of other parents have probably found it too. You can go to enormous lengths to meet the admissions criteria but still find demand for places is much greater than supply. We are supposed to have a choice about where we send our children to school, but this is not everybody's experience.

It's not uncommon for families to choose where they live and work based around where their children will be educated.

Parents with no religious leanings will start going to church if that is what it takes to get a church school place. Many private schools in the UK will take your child's name on their waiting list from birth. In both private and state sectors, the demand for places in the best schools is tough, competitive, and stressful for both parents and children. Your child is likely to spend the next 13 years in school so you want to feel you have done your best to make a good choice for them. There are so many factors involved here – again, worthy of an entire book! A good place to start, like with choosing childcare, is to first work out in your own mind what you're looking for in a school and what's important to you. What kind of an education do you want your children to have? Plus, who else is involved in the decision? Your partner? The children's father? Grandparents if they've offered to pay school fees?

The good news is that you can think about the questions you need to consider and start gathering your answers well ahead of time. There is no such thing as the perfect school because schools are not run by machines. Also, you may still have very young children and not be in a position yet to know what kind of a school will suit their character or special needs.

Here are some good questions to get you thinking. They are divided into primary and secondary, as your needs or your child's may be quite different by the time you require a secondary school. For example, you might be quite happy to send your son or daughter to the local state primary, but you feel strongly that single sex education is what you want for their secondary education.

What's important to me in choosing a primary school?
e.g. It must be local, or it has to have a great sports curriculum and facilities, or it must be a church school

What's important to me in choosing a secondary school?

Looking at what you have written, do you feel your answers are or will be relevant for all your children? Is there anything that would be particularly important for one of your children, such as special needs or music facilities? If so, put that child's initial beside that item on your list.

Having considered the needs of your children, which would you say is the **most** important thing to you when choosing a school?

If your husband/partner/children's father were to complete this exercise, what would you do if he had very different priorities to you? For example, one of you might want to pay for education, whereas the other may be fiercely against this.

Is answering these questions helping you to identify what kind of schools you want to consider? It's vital that you're choosing a school that will be a good match for your family, not just one child, because you will live with this for years. For example, having one child at a school with a long journey time will have an impact on everyone else in the family. At the same time, individual needs will have to be taken into consideration. It might be that your children can, or have to, go to the same schools but keep an open mind – the world will not end if you need to find different schools to suit your children's needs. Over time, schools and children change and they might not always be the best fit for each other. If your child becomes increasingly unhappy, you need to feel satisfied that their current school has done everything they can to help your child before deciding to move schools. Equally, they could just have a bumpy term with a new teacher, so try and take a longer view (not easy if it's your first child) and take into account siblings, location, ethos and friendships before deciding to change schools.

Taking time to sort out your educational values is not wasted. There is no point in choosing a school with a strong homework policy if you think homework is a waste of time – you're likely to have a long battle on your hands.

I thought our school worries were over having finally found a primary school we were happy with, until a friend started the process of looking for secondary schools and the whole nightmare returned with a vengeance.

Laura, two children

Assessing a school

You can find out about schools by reading their brochure or website, visiting them and talking to existing parents and children. Best of all, do all three and anything else you can think of to reach a decision. There are Ofsted reports and schools' guides for both private and state schools. Other parents' views are helpful, but you are likely to find a mix of good and bad experiences. The brochure can look very impressive, but does the school really match up to that? Find out when they are having an open day, but it is also valuable to arrange to see a school on an ordinary day too, when all the children are there to learn. You get a much better picture of a typical school day this way. When you meet the headteacher, it is your job to interview them, not the other way round. Here are some good questions you can ask:

- How large are your classes?
- Do you offer before- and after-school care?
- Do you specialize in certain areas (such as art or sport)?
- How do you cater for children with special learning or health needs?
- How do you ensure the children make friends?
- Do you have an anti-bullying strategy and a health and welfare programme?
- How do you ensure the children are safe in the playground and the toilets?
- Do you have an intervention and extension programme in literacy and numeracy?
- Do you respect and support children's cultural and ethnic backgrounds?
- What are your policies on homework/discipline/assessment?
- Do you cater for low-income families (reduced levies, low-cost excursions)?
- Do you encourage parental involvement?

What would you like to ask a school?

You need to balance the answers you receive to these questions, but most of all ask yourself this: does your heart, your mind or your gut give you a good feeling about the school? Can you imagine your child being happy there? If they are not happy, then they won't learn.

Preparing for school

Transition to school can be easy for some children and a battle for others. As a mother, you are a huge influence on how your children will feel about starting school or changing schools. Mothers are inclined to worry about practicalities such as having the right uniform and how long the school run will take. Then there are emotional issues such as will their child make friends or like their teacher? Being anxious or agitated is not helpful to our children.

The happier you can make the transition the more positive the child feels about it.

Raising Happy Children, Jan Parker and Jan Stimpson

It's the little things that can make a big difference. Have a look at these top tips from other mothers to ease the way for you and your child to start school.

- Find out if you can meet up with other families who are also starting the school and arrange a play date.
- Prepare them to follow instructions using prepositions such as 'under', 'beside' and 'next to' – teachers will say 'Come and line up, stand behind Johnny'. So, make this kind of thing easy for your child to follow, this helps prevent them feeling nervous or unsure.
- Talk to them about a school day in simple terms – too much detail is bewildering. Buy books about starting school or do role plays about starting school, act them out with your child or use dolls or toys.
- Ask the teacher how the child is supposed to ask about going to the toilet and whether they will be expected to shut the door. Will they have to sit at a desk? This kind of detail can help a child to know how to behave and it could be different from what's OK at home.
- If they are having school lunch find out what they're expected to eat or if it is monitored. If your child will take a packed lunch, agree with them what things will be going in their lunch box and what to eat first.

- Buy easy clothes and shoes to take on and off (Velcro, not laces).
- Label everything! Use a laundry marker pen if you don't want to sew in labels.
- Choose a fun school bag and lunch box with your child.
- The school will have a view on how long parents can stay in a classroom to help settle their child – try and stick to what the school needs but if your child is really unhappy then discuss this with their teacher, but not when your child is listening.
- If your child's first day or so is fraught, don't dismiss the intensity of their feelings. Do you remember your own first day? Let your child know you understand and give them reassurance that it's OK to feel unhappy. Emphasize what is positive about school and that you have faith they will be fine.
- Some children are fine for a week or two and then the penny drops that this school business is here to stay, and they go right off it. You will need to ride the waves with them and be aware that they're likely to be really exhausted too as they adjust. They might be grumpy or fed up at home after having to be 'good' all day at school.
- Age matters – a child, especially a boy, is likely to need more support to cope with the rigours of the school day when they have only just turned four than others in the class who are about to turn five. A year is a very long time at this age and if you can let your child start school a bit later in the year it could mean they settle in better.

If my daughter was having an 'off' day, I would pop a simple note in her lunch box to let her know I was still thinking about her as she ate her sandwiches.

Janice, three children under 16 years old

Getting involved

You have chosen a school to educate and look after your children and yet how much do you know about what goes on there? Your child might not be the most reliable source of information. Teachers are very busy people, and may not see it as their job to help you feel part of the school community. Most schools *will* welcome some kind of parental involvement. Not only do you get to see more of the school in action, but your children will love having you there on a school trip or to help with reading. If you are a mother with young children, and you have not gone back to full-time work, then this is a great time to support the school. By the time your children have moved on to secondary schools, most mothers have returned to work, and finding time to support the school is much harder. Also, if you have been active on the parents' committee or fundraising, it can be a bonus on your CV.

Ways to be involved:

- Classroom – reading, helping on special school days like sports or science days.
- School trips – accompanying your child's class on outings, your child will love it!
- Parents' association – class rep or committee member.
- Fundraising – organize events, or just turn up and help out on a stall.
- Hold a coffee morning for the parents in your class to build friendships.
- Organize an end of summer term picnic.
- Do you have a skill or a job that could be of interest to the children?
- Charity – suggest a favourite charity the school could support and offer to run the campaign or supply promotional materials.
- Attend events – school plays and concerts, summer fair/Christmas bazaar, red nose day etc.
- Thank/Praise a teacher – they are doing an incredibly important job and they need to be rewarded and not just contacted when you have a problem.

We had moved to a new town in order to give our children a great place to grow up with excellent local schools. Not long after we had moved, I went to my daughter's class parents' coffee morning which I was dreading to be honest, as I am quite shy. The other mothers all knew each other really well, but they were so friendly to me it was hard to stay feeling shy for long. It made such a difference the next day dropping my daughter off as I felt far more connected to the other mums and the school.

Laura, two children, ten and seven years old when they moved

Friendships

Since when did we model our conduct on that of other people?

Laurie Orr

A large part of childhood includes friends, and many of them are made at school and that is why friendship is in this part of the book. Friends are hugely influential on your children, and you will find that you can become very opinionated about them. The ones you like or don't like, the ones you resent, and the ones that make you anxious. They will be in your house frequently, and your children will go to their house too. Many discussions will result between you and your child about their friends. At some point you are likely to be told you are the meanest mother in the world because, unlike Sam's mum, you won't give your child pudding every day, the latest toy, or a TV in their bedroom. Remember that parents get themselves into awful knots over trying to be fair, but we live in an unfair world. It's not fair that Africa has 12 million orphaned children, or that some children are living with alcoholic or drug-dependent parents who forget they exist. As children enter their teens, friends can become even more influential than parents and it is never too soon to be aware of this, but you decide how much of that influence you are prepared to have in the family. Remember, you get to choose your friends but not your family.

The meaning of friendship – through the ages

Here's a rough guide to what friendship means according to the age of a child in their first ten years. It is a *rough* guide, and other factors are very important, such as personality, gender, family circumstances and birth order.

Age 0–2

Some recognition that the other child exists. Some early squabbles about toys or possessions. Some affection which might not be welcome!

Meeting up with a friend is probably more beneficial to the parents than the babies.

Age 3–7

A playmate (but not for very long). At this age a friend is someone who helps you, but it probably wouldn't occur to you to help them. You might argue or fight and an adult will probably have to help you resolve your battles. You begin to play at their house without your mummy being there too. You might even stay the night!

Age 6–10
You do help each other out. You share and take turns. You mainly play with same-sex friends. The 'best' friend idea is present. If you fall out, even a minor setback can be a tragedy.

If you want to find out more about the ages and stages of friendships, go to the Taking it further section.

No friends and unkind friends

It is heartbreaking for mothers when they see their child having difficulties making friends. Some children are naturally shy, or content with their own company. Perhaps it is our problem, not theirs, that they have few or no friends. Think about yourself or your partner? Do you have lots of friends or are you quite shy too? Our children pick up our behaviour, so if you're standing in the corner of the playground quietly hoping no one will talk to you, then what is the message you are sending your child?

What memories do you have about friendships when you were a child (under 10)?

How do those memories influence your view on your child's friendships?

If you have concerns about your child not making or keeping friends, here are some ideas that could help your child:

- Make an effort to talk to other parents at school – this encourages children to get to know each other.
- Find local activities where your child will have opportunities to make friends outside of school, such as cubs, a drama group or swimming lessons.

- Encourage your child – talk to them about friendships, share memories of your childhood friends and ask your child about their view of friends.
- Teach social skills and sociable behaviour – explain to your child how to understand non-verbal and verbal cues, for example, someone smiling at him or making a jokey remark.
- Your child may overreact to teasing, or may pressure others to play when they've said 'No'.
- Take the time to use role play to show your child, for example, how to make eye contact and to smile to show he's being friendly. Your child could also practise saying something like, 'Hello, I'm Jake, would you like to play?'
- Teach basic social rules – not to snatch things or hit others, and how to share and cooperate.
- Avoid 'showing up' your child or telling them off in front of friends – if their behaviour is unacceptable take them to one side and be clear about how you want their behaviour to stop or change.
- Teach negotiation and conflict resolution – talk to your child about how to listen to others, state his point of view assertively and how to compromise.
- Listen to any mention of bullying. Find out what the school's policy is and deal with it. Bullying can have lifelong consequences, so take it seriously.
- Equally, friendships do blow up and down in the space of a break time, so make sure you are reading the signals from your child's mood and behaviour to determine if there is a persistent problem with friends.
- Cuddle and show warmth. This is invaluable as it helps boost your child's confidence, if there are friendship difficulties.

'Unsuitable' friends

I was amazed at the kind of people who became our friends after we had children, and the friends we already had who, once they became parents, we found it harder to socialize with. Either our children didn't get on, or we were shocked at what they let their children do. We went away for a weekend with some lovely old friends we don't see much of as they moved away and it was very tense. They had such different rules to us. They were very liberal with their kids and had no rules about meals or bedtimes, and of course our kids thought it was fantastic to eat crisps all evening and stay up late. My husband and I found it upsetting and tiring re-negotiating with our children all weekend, and I don't think we will be in a hurry to go away with that family again. I would never have thought that we would have such a different approach to parenting.

Lizzie two children, five and three years old

This mother was away for a weekend with another family, which is a long stretch of time if you find your parenting values are clashing head on. Even a short after-school playtime or a chat with another mum at a baby group can leave you feeling unsure about the other mother's parenting values. If your child is going to play in someone else's house, then you will want to feel confident that he or she will be happy, safe and nurtured there, not exposed to ideas or behaviours that worry you. Trust your gut instinct as well as any evidence you have that you are not happy to let your child spend time with that family.

Here are some top tips from other mothers who have been faced with the unsuitable friends dilemma.

When you have a baby and you meet other mums, don't be surprised if you notice how everyone can have very different standards and values about how they are looking after their baby.

Laura, two children

It depends on the age of your child. When they're under five, you have much more control over who they are spending time with. Once they start nursery or school, and receive invitations to play at other people's houses, you realize how much you care about them not being exposed to different values.

Susie, one child

Be very careful about banning a friend as this is likely to make them more interesting and attractive to your child.

Jane, two children

Stick to your gut instinct. Your child might be unhappy about you not wanting them to play with a friend you're unsure about. Suggest they come and play at your house so you can get to know the child better and make everyone welcome in your home.

Janice, three children

Sleepovers – or 'no sleep-overs' as we call them! We have a house rule that our kids can't sleep over unless we know the family and we are happy with the arrangements.

June, three children

Drip your values in... 'In our house we eat at the table and say please and thank you, or we play with friends, not watch TV'.

Louise, two children

I was amazed at how much our values have rubbed off. Our kids do recognize when a friend is not treating them nicely or is being rude to adults. I'm glad I held my tongue on a number of occasions and didn't judge their friends for them.

Laura, three children

Friends will be a source of joy and at times pain to your children. They are a natural and important part of growing up. As mothers, we are influential in the way our children make and keep friends, and the effort you put in now to teach them the basic rules of friendship will help them to develop into kind and valued friends themselves, whatever their age.

Education isn't just about schools

A child's academy is his mother's knee.

James Russell Lowell

In spite of the many years your child will be spending in school, parents are still the biggest influence on how we turn out as adults – capable of being creative, earning a living, and making relationships.

As Freud said, 'Love and work, work and love, that's all there is'. You are your child's gatekeeper to the world, and you are capable of offering them all kinds of learning that they won't find in the classroom. During their first ten years, a child is like a huge sponge soaking up gallons of experiences and learning. Whatever your practical or financial circumstances, you have boundless potential for enriching their learning from day one.

By being in a family, children learn the foundations of how to function in society.

Mothers, if they only realized it, are still the pivotal force in their families, teaching many skills that can really only be learned by the osmosis of day-to-day living.

Where a school has to teach to a prescribed curriculum, mothers teach through a desire to fine tune their child's physical, emotional, social, and cultural well-being. She will also pass on fountains of incidental knowledge, giving the child a sense of their own history and place in the family. A mother can teach the child about love and how to cherish people in their own family above all else.

Liz Scott, Montessori Educator (three grown-up children)

Think about what you learnt at your mother's knee? The difference between right and wrong? How to make things – from a birthday card to a Sunday roast? Or how to sew on a button or be kind to a neighbour? We know we inherit our parents' values and some of us are keen to reject them. But in the ordinary fog of day-to-day life as a mother, your children are learning practically, emotionally and creatively from you all the time. They watch how you butter toast, answer the phone, cuddle a tearful baby and write a loving message in a birthday card all at the same time. In addition, outside of school hours, you have probably organized their hobbies too – toddler club, Brownies or football has to be sorted out by someone and it's usually mothers because we want our children to broaden their lives and have these opportunities (we also want them out of the house and worn out!). Think about the following questions.

How am I already expanding my children's education in terms of:

Values
e.g. teaching them manners

Practical skills
e.g. showing them how to lay a table

Hobbies and interests
e.g. organizing for them to play instruments or taking them swimming

Too much in the diary?

Meet the Johnson children. Jade is nine, Tom is six and Lucy is three. This is their typical week during term time.

Monday: Lucy – toddler club, Tom – football

Tuesday: Lucy – baby gym, Tom – karate, Jade – Brownies

Wednesday: Lucy – park with a friend, Tom – maths tutor, Jade – flute

Thursday: Lucy – toddler swimming, Tom and Jade – kids club

Friday: Lucy – friend to play, Tom – friend to play, Jade – swimming

Saturday: Tom – swimming, Jade – jazz

Sunday: see Granny, homework, get ready for school.

Do you see any space in this week for these children to simply just be at home?

> *I just don't think an hour of piano, followed by an hour of ballet, followed by an hour of God-knows-what makes them a better person.*

Kate Winslet, actress and mum of two

It is really good for children to be bored sometimes, and not have all their spare time organized for them. In boredom, we give space for creativity to emerge. A child who says 'Mummy, I'm bored' and is greeted with suggestions of what to do and lots of parental input will get the message that telling mummy they are bored means that mummy will fix the problem. Instead, empathize with the feeling, but encourage the child to resource *themselves* and to tell you when they have come up with something to do. Say to them, 'Being bored is frustrating. What can you do about it? When you've decided, come and tell me.'

For younger children, they will need more guidance or distraction, and they may not even know the word 'bored', but you will be able to tell by their behaviour if they are bored! The point is that children need to feel resourceful and capable of creating their own entertainment. Some children find this easier than others – often second or subsequent children. Firstborn children have had your exclusive attention for however many years before baby number two arrived so they can find it harder to entertain themselves.

What do you really want to teach your children?

You might be sitting reading this book with your first baby tucked up beside you. Or maybe you have several children. Wherever you are on the journey into motherhood, take a moment and think about the opportunities you have, or could have, to teach them and offer them experiences during these precious first ten years of their lives. You might want to switch off the phone and invest about 20 minutes in the exercise below.

What do I want to teach my children?
e.g. the importance of working hard or the value of friendship

What experiences do I want to provide for them?
e.g. to travel as widely as possible or to mix with all kinds of people

What resources will I/we need to provide these experiences?

What's the most significant thing my mother taught me that I would like to pass on to my children?

My mother was great at being warm and friendly, but it wasn't until I left home and got married that I learnt how to iron a shirt. Did it matter? No, not really, her warmth was what I treasured and I want my kids to be more concerned about warmth and friendliness than perfectly ironed shirts.

Lara, three children

Learning log

Check you are happy that you have learnt each point below and feel ready to apply it to your life.

- Understand your childcare options.
- Know what is important to you about childcare.
- Recognize the importance of building a good relationship with your child carer.
- Know how to settle your child.
- Consider what's important to you about choosing a school.
- Be prepared for school.
- Know how to get involved with your school.
- Understand the impact of friendship.
- Acknowledge that you are your child's main teacher.

What have I learnt about myself as a mother by reading this chapter?

What is the most significant thing?

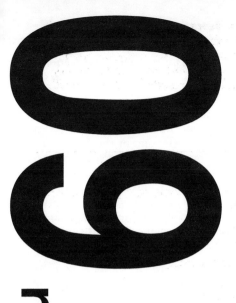

09

running a family

In this chapter you will learn:
- how to get on top of daily family life
- the importance of a health check
- about a conducive home environment
- how to deal with changes as children grow older.

To do carefully and consistently and kindly many little things, is not a little thing.

Stephen Covey, *The Seven Habits o Highly Effective Families*

Do you feel like you have to be superwoman to be a mother and run a home and family? There are so many things to think about – often simultaneously. Your mind flits between the physical, practical and emotional needs of everyone in the family. You will be aware that you've run out of milk, that your daughter has been a bit quiet lately and that the dog needs a walk in a heartbeat. Mothers are both the engines and the drivers of a car we'll call 'The Family' that could break down or go off-road without warning, and at that point the mother is also the mechanic. She's also the fuel in the engine too and sometimes she's running on empty.

Family life is very demanding and just when you think you have got things in reasonably good shape, something changes. One person grows up a bit, or another goes through a bad patch. Someone being ill for a few days can drag the family down into a murky soup of snotty tissues and too much TV. You might have a major event like a new baby, a bereavement or a house move which may trigger the 'Family Car' to go off the road again for a while. It's perfectly normal to feel swamped by the challenge of running a family. Every family in the world has good and bad days. This chapter will help you get to grips with all that's involved in keeping your family running smoothly, without you reaching for the vodka bottle!

All day, every day

As a mother, you are directly or partially responsible for your children and the home they are growing up in. If you have a partner, you are also responsible for your part in that relationship as well as many other relationships. Do you have any pets in the house? Who thinks about their welfare? Who notices they need feeding, walking or cleaning out? Most likely the mother in the household, although she might have struck a successful deal with her children to see that these jobs are done. What about holidays – who thinks about and plans them? How about birthdays and other celebrations? Recycling, is that part of your family's habits, and if so, who is making sure the cardboard and the bottles go in the right bins and are put out on the right night of the week?

The diary. Such a little word, but to busy mothers it contains a huge amount of content that needs managing and balancing every day. Food, from ingredients to tasty suppers, takes planning and skill – who is doing that in your house? Anyone got first-aid training? If not, being a mother will certainly give you the opportunity to learn on the job as you stick on a plaster or escort an injured child to the hospital.

Are you feeling under the weather too? Sorry, no such thing as sick leave for mothers.

Tasklist

These issues are typical of most households, so have a look at the list on the next pages and tick which apply to you and add any of your own at the end. Look at the categories and then write who in your family is doing this most – is it you, your partner, your childcarer or someone else?

When *you* do these tasks, how does it make you feel? One mum said she loves ironing her children's clothes, but finds cooking really tedious. Another said she was quite happy to take her children for doctor's appointments, but she couldn't cope with the dentist. What follows here is a very long list of jobs that get done in families, but who is doing them? If it's you, to what extent are all these jobs a joy or a burden?

In the column about feelings, use a numbering scale to gauge the strength of your feelings. For example 1 would mean you can't stand the task, 2 means it's okay, and 3 means you enjoy it.

Here are a couple of examples to help you get the idea:

Household budget – I do it – 2
Family shopping – My partner does it – 1 (I hate supermarkets)
Taking kids to school – I do it – 3 (I love it)

> 1 = you loathe it
> 2 = you don't mind it
> 3 = you enjoy it

What area of family life	Who does this the most?	Feelings score
Childcare – general		
Getting them up		
Taking them to/from school		
Social arrangements with friends		
Taking them to sports/ hobbies		
Cooking and feeding them		
Entertaining them		
Bathing them		
Putting them to bed		
Discipline		
School involvement		
Shopping for clothes, shoes etc.		
The diary		
Organizing your time		
Organizing your children and family's time		
Holidays		
Planning		

Booking		
Packing		
Finance		
Budget		
Management		
Insurance policies		
Home		
Shopping		
Cooking		
Cleaning		
Rubbish and recycling		
Laundry		
Gardening		
DIY repairs		
Sorting and tidying		
Technology – computer, TV, mobiles etc.		
Birthdays/Celebrations		
Planning parties		
Shopping		
Managing and doing		
Religion		
Observing special days and rituals		
Practising – (going to church, synagogue, mosque etc.)		
Pet care		
Feeding		
Exercising		

Health		
Doctor visits		
Dentist visits		
Care at home		
Nutrition		
Other		

There are over 40 categories in this table and each one could be analyzed again in terms of what it entails and how it is dealt with. Multi-tasking is a modern cliché, but how else can we describe what is going on in a mother's mind, heart and hands? The 'job spec' of being a mother is endless, and not defined, but what is clear is that you are doing an enormous amount every day, and much of this is unrewarded. This is just the practical day-to-day stuff of running a family, this is not including the emotional side of mothering, and yet this list alone is enough to make anyone need a holiday!

What was your total score?

40–60 = running a family is more of a burden than a joy

60–90 = running a family brings you pleasure and pain

90–120 = you are a domestic goddess – who wouldn't want to live with you?

How do you feel now looking at the way you have filled in this table?

What about your scores – any surprises?

Let's take a look at the tasks that scored one point, because these are the areas that you are not enjoying and finding a challenge.

Your five most hated chores

Have a look at the top five areas of practical family life that really drive you mad – for which you scored one. Choose the ones that would have the most positive effect on you, or your children, if you made some changes.

Write them here.

1.

2.

3.

4.

5.

What would you like to change about each area? Remember, it needs to be something that is within your control. For example, if you are the one who hates doing the family shop (like the mother below),what is it that you find a challenge? Wondering what to buy? Making a list? The shopping trip itself? Spending money? The whole consumer spending frenzy you see in the supermarket?

I hate shopping. I find it boring and annoying trying to think of different meals to make and what to buy, so I put it off for as long as possible. I have tried online shopping and it's okay, but not perfect. Supermarkets make me really fed up so wherever possible I use the local shops, which makes me feel a bit better about it. As a single mum I accept that until my kids are a bit older they can't help me out – so instead of dreading it I now just try to get on with it and see it as a part of the requirements of being a mum.

Laura, two children, six and three years old

Having identified specifically what you find challenging, what changes could you make to help you cope better with these parts of family life?

My challenge	What can I do about it	What support I need
e.g. Cleaning the house	Clean up one room a day, not leave everything to do at the weekend.	Tell the children and get them to help.

A typical day

Love is a four letter word spelt T-I-M-E.

Lorraine Thomas

You're a mother so you are already a time management expert (although you probably have days when that is the opposite of how you would describe yourself)! From today, commit to thinking of yourself as a mother who is on top of the diary and at ease with managing your time. You can do this and you owe it to yourself to make a typical day run smoothly. Of course there will be unexpected events like illness or accidents, or just days when you simply can't be bothered, but use this opportunity to overhaul your typical family day and see what a difference you can make to your stress levels. Feeling stressed is a terrible energy drain, so by making your day less stressful you will have more energy – are you up for that?

The clock

Mothers often say: 'I've run out of time', 'There's no time to fit everything in', 'I don't know where the time's gone', 'Hurry up', 'There's no time to do that now', 'I'm sorry we're late again', 'You'll be late'.

Consider what the over-riding effect is, on *you* hearing yourself saying these things repeatedly?

What is the effect on your children when they hear you say these things?

> **What phrases do you say on a regular a basis, indicating that time has got the better of you?**

There are only 24 hours in a day, and nothing is going to change that. If you keep running out of time to do things, are you taking on too much, or are you taking longer and perhaps more care than is necessary over what you are doing? Where is all your time going on a typical day?

Look at the tasks below that happen all the time in families. Tick the ones you have in your typical day, and add any that are not included.

Daily checklist

Sleeping	☐
Bathing	☐
Housework	☐
Shopping/running errands	☐
Looking after your children (dressing, bathing, feeding, supervising)	☐
Playing, reading or having fun with your children	☐
Travelling to work	☐
Working	☐
Cooking	☐
Relaxing (watching TV or reading)	☐
E-mail and phone	☐
Time with your partner	☐
Time for yourself	☐

Now, look at this 24-hour table and put in how much time you spend (approximately) on each activity. It's in two hourly sections.

Day	How much time are you spending on each activity? Use the ones on your typical daily checklist on page 199
6am–8am	
8am–10am	
10am–noon	
Noon–2pm	
2pm–4pm	
4pm–6pm	
Night	
6pm–8pm	
8pm–10pm	
10pm–midnight	
Midnight-6am	

Which are the times in the day when you feel the most stressed? And the least (apart from when you are actually asleep)?

How much time are you currently spending with your children having fun, playing or reading to them when they have your undivided attention?

How much 'Me' time is there?

Stress pinnacle

Highlight the most stressful hours of your typical day.

What is causing the stress for you at these times? It's very easy for families to get stuck in ruts and assume that our typical days will remain just that. But, as a mother, your life is so full, so why put up with stressful mornings or evenings when you could make some changes. This mother chose to do something about stress levels on school mornings.

My mornings were hideous – everyone shouting at each other and no one listening. Nothing was in the right place and my husband would be the only one eating his breakfast in peace while I ran round like a headless chicken simultaneously mopping up spilled cereal and shoving children into coats and shoes while barking instructions into the air. I had to believe that we could do better than this; it could hardly be any worse. It's obvious now, but it never occurred to me how much time (and tempers!) could be saved by making packed lunches the night before, and insisting that the children sorted out their school bags. Also, I decided that instead of leaving the kitchen perfect, it was good enough to just pile everything in the sink and deal with it later. Our mornings are a lot calmer now, and I feel better about it because I chose to control the mornings instead of letting them control me. Plus, the children have noticed that I am more relaxed. Before we all say goodbye for the day I want us to be on good terms. I used to see in their eyes they were pleased to see the back of their screaming mother.

Jane, two children under ten years old

The success of transforming your most stressful times in the day will be down to paying attention to the detail and being ruthless about what is necessary.

Over the next two days (choose whether you want to look at: weekdays or weekends – whatever is most stressful for you and keep a record of what you are *actually* doing every 15 minutes. You won't have to do this forever, but it will be worth it to see where your time is going.

Below is a chart to help you. It gives you three hours in 15-minute intervals (so adapt it if you find one hour or more than three hours is what you want to investigate). Begin by filling in the first two columns with the hours you want to improve, and what is going on at the moment for every 15 minutes.

Leave the last column blank for now.

My most stressful time of the day		
Time slot every 15 minutes	What I am doing	What I want to do
e.g. 7.00 am –7.15	In shower, getting dressed	

Now, if you could start again with this most stressful time of your typical day, what changes would you make to ease the stress? Make sure they are within your control, (wishing you could employ an au pair to do everything might not be possible).

Is it time to start getting the family to share the load with you? Giving children responsibility is great for their self-esteem as well as teaching them a life skill. You might have to put up with their version of a made bed or a soggy sandwich, but it is a step on their road to independence. It's understandable to think it will be quicker and easier if you do it yourself, but you are making a rod for you own back and you are not their servant. At what point will you think it is time to pass on these skills to your children?

Jot down your ideas and then come up with your revised version of your time usage in the remaining column. It's up to you to put this into action. No one else can do this for you, but you might want to ask for some support from your family during this adjustment process. They might moan and groan, but remind them of the benefits of a more relaxed mother, so it's in their interest to cooperate with this new regime. When will you start?

Food, glorious food

What is it about mothers and food? Before you had children, what was your relationship with food and cooking like? How is it different now you are a mother? It used to be so easy only having to think about yourself or you and your partner, but with children, the pressure is on to be a nutrition expert and a gourmet cook. And it's relentless, the fridge empties out far quicker than you want it to and to make matters worse, it's alarming how much food is wasted and thrown away.

Before I had kids I used to love trying out new recipes and having friends round for dinner. Now I find it a huge bore having to churn out family meals that are nutritious and also take into account the fussy eaters and the fact that my partner is vegetarian. The responsibility of organizing family meals 21 times a week has damaged my passion for food and cooking. Even if we get a takeaway or eat out, I still feel that I am the one weighing up whether we do that or not.

Susie, two daughters, eight and five years old

Here are some other pressures that mothers experience around food and cooking for the family:

- Catering for everyone's tastes and/or allergies.
- Shopping efficiently.

- Offering variety.
- Providing fruit and vegetables.
- Buying organic produce where possible.
- Being careful about fat, salt and sugar content.
- Knowing about E numbers, additives and preservatives.
- Using up leftovers.
- Eating more fish and vegetarian dishes, and less red meat.
- Cooking fresh meals, not ready meals.
- Drinking plenty of water.
- Being mindful of alcohol consumption.
- Following recipes and expanding recipe repertoires.
- Knowing how to make party food and cakes.
- Having enough food for everyone.
- Managing portion size.
- Watching my own weight and anyone else's that concerns me.

From the day your baby is born you cannot escape from a vast world of advice and information about what to feed your child. Breastfeed or bottle-feed, when to start solids, what foods to avoid or even why red smarties are evil. The link between food, behaviour and learning can be on your mind as you write your shopping list or decide what to cook for tea. How you manage cooking and feeding your family will depend on your own relationship with food and your experience of food as a child. Allergies are on the increase, so you may have no choice about certain foods, or you might dread mealtimes as one or more of your children make them a nightmare. It's bewildering and exhausting, but you can't escape from the need to feed your children. If you find the whole area overwhelming, what would make it easier for you? Start by identifying what you find most challenging about food and meals. Then, identify what you find enjoyable. Finally, what would you like to do to change your relationship with food and mealtimes that would make it better for you?

What do you find challenging about providing food for your family?

What do you find enjoyable about it?

What changes would you like to make to improve food and mealtimes?

Early on we equate being a good mother with how we feed our children. You're a 'good mother' if you feed your kids healthy food.

Goldie Alfashi

Feelings within the family

A mother is someone who cries when you have done something bad, and cries even harder when you have done something good.

Robin Di Biase, age 14

Feelings are everywhere in families but it's likely to be the mother's emotional state that affects the rest of the family. Happy mothers fill their homes with a spirit of optimism, the sound of laughter and their children's artwork. Confident mothers tackle problems head on, instead of being swamped by them. But what if you struggle with being a mother, or you have low self-esteem? Do you live with a difficult partner or perhaps you are on your own? Whatever creates your mood, it can be like a plug stopping the flow of a happy atmosphere. It's not about who's at fault – who doesn't have days when the grey cloud descends and we just want everyone to go away? Take seriously the fact that the mood of the mother underpins the atmosphere and the behaviour in the family. Of course, fathers have their part to play too, but this book is about motherhood – what a responsibility!

Do you identify with any of these comments?

Sometimes my mood becomes everyone else's. I'm aware of how much control I have over the atmosphere in the house. If I'm in a grump, then all the routine things like tidying away toys or making supper make me snappy and then the children snap back at me. I end up shouting at them to stop shouting – how crazy is that?

Sarah, three children

My friend is one of those mums who has the potatoes for dinner peeled and sitting in cold water before breakfast is over. I just about make sure the baby is fed and changed and the children have consumed something vaguely healthy before I take them to school. I try not to feel intimidated by other mothers' organizational skills, but it is hard.

Rose, three children

If my husband and I are happy and communicating well with each other then I can put up with a lot more challenges as a mother.

Natalie, four children

I made an effort to wash the kitchen floor before my mother-in-law came for the weekend. Shortly after her arrival, we were chatting in the kitchen and she said 'Now, you put your feet up and I'll wash the kitchen floor for you.' My heart sank; my standards were just not good enough for her, but I just let her get on with it, she meant well.

Caris, three children

The importance of a mother's mood

Studies show how a mother's mood has a fundamental impact on bonding with her newborn baby and affects its development. Every day your emotional world will continue to govern what kind of a day you have and what kind of a day your children have too. So much has already been written about the importance of a mother's feelings in this book and many other books. Can you appreciate how important it is to take your feelings seriously?

Confidence is the number one obstacle for mothers to be able to thrive and cope with the practical demands of running a family.

Go back again and see what you wrote in Chapter 01 about your own levels of confidence.

How do you feel now about what you learnt in Chapter 01? Also, Chapters 02 and 03 on family values and family relationships are just as integral to how you deal with the practicalities of family life, so check again what you discovered in those chapters by looking at the learning log pages at the end of each one. Below are some questions for you to consider.

What feelings do I experience that alter my ability to run the family?

Positive feelings:
e.g. pride or happiness

Negative feelings:
e.g. anger or boredom

What influences the way I feel about running the family?
e.g. tiredness or PMT

Your feelings are genuine, and you cannot control them arriving, but you *can* choose how you respond to them without reducing their significance. It's perfectly normal to have an 'off day' so don't sweep your feelings under the carpet and pretend everything is fine. Your children will sense there is something not quite right about you. Role modelling emotional intelligence (being able to manage your emotions) to them is a brilliant life skill to pass on. State how you are feeling clearly, without blaming or shaming anyone.

Shouting doesn't work when I'm angry. I'm getting better at being aware that I'm starting to boil, so I'll say to the kids I'm really angry about this so I'm going outside to calm down and then we'll talk about it.

Lucy, three children

Avoiding labels

Remember it's OK to feel cross about behaviour but say how you feel without labelling or attacking the person. A label is a single word used to describe someone, but it doesn't give the person much information about what they have done, and it sticks. It becomes self-fulfilling. If you keep telling a child they are 'good' or 'rude' or 'naughty', that's what they will be.

For example, instead of saying, 'You're so naughty to draw on the wall', why nor try 'I'm cross that that there is drawing on the wall. In our house we draw on paper'. Notice how this also directs the child with what is acceptable – drawing on paper. Look at these typical sentences that parents say and rewrite them describing the behaviour or what you see, without using labels.

---

1. You clumsy girl; you spilt your juice!

2. You're so good.

3. You're a helpful boy. You put the toys away.

4. You are naughty children throwing the Lego around.

Using respectful clear communication like this will help you stay on top of your feelings. It will also boost your confidence as you take control of unacceptable behaviour. Keep labels for jars, not for people.

Health check

If you live off crisps, wine and chocolate, and take the car to post a letter then do you think your energy levels will be high enough to run a family?

Every week there are surveys and reports about healthy living, obesity and lack of exercise being responsible for a whole range of problems in children and families. From education to concentration, our children are not performing and much of this is down to an unhealthy diet and not enough exercise. This can add to a mother's guilt and there is already so much to cope with that trying to eat well and live a healthy lifestyle is just another pressure. This chapter is not written to make you feel worse, but to inspire you to take a look at how your family is running. Your physical state will have an impact on your ability to run the family, so what could you do to make it easier to be healthy? There are endless books, websites, magazines and TV programmes to help you learn about healthy living – so lack of information is not the problem. The problem is more likely to be connected to your energy levels, will power and your image of yourself. Do you think you are worth taking good care of? Of course you are! Being able to cope with motherhood will be easier if you are in good physical condition. You don't need to be a size ten, but if your energy levels are struggling to keep up with the demands of family life, then how about making some changes?

Ask yourself these questions:

1 What does being healthy mean to you?
2 How healthy are you compared to how you would like to be?
3 What about the family?
4 If you ate a more balanced diet and had regular exercise, what would the benefits be to you and your family?

This is not a scientific survey nor a book dedicated to healthy living, but have a go at the health check below.

Nutrition	Mostly	Sometimes	Rarely
I eat a well-balanced diet			
I eat red meat less than five times a week			
I eat five portions of fruit and veg a day			
I prepare fresh meals			
I eat ready meals			
I drink less than 15 units of alcohol a week			
I eat chocolate daily			
I eat cake or biscuits daily			
I drink more than one litre of water a day			
I drink less than five cups of tea or coffee a day			
Exercise			
I am out of breath for 20 minutes 3 times per week			
I take regular exercise			
I exercise with my family			
I play a sport			
I walk or cycle wherever possible			
I use stairs instead of escalators or lifts			

Time to make changes?

Looking at your results, in what way would you like to make some changes to your diet and exercise regime? Don't aim for perfection, but think of all the benefits you would experience if you had more energy?

Changes I would like to make to my diet and exercise regime...

Finally, think of seven achievable but significant steps you could take in the next seven days to make a positive difference to your lifestyle. Aim for one a day and keep it simple – eat an extra piece of fruit, drink one more glass of water, park the car ten minutes walk away from the school – you choose.

Seven steps to a healthier week

Day 1

Day 2

Day 3

Day 4

Day 5

Day 6

Day 7

Remember, your children are watching you! Why should they eat less chocolate biscuits and more fruit unless they see you doing the same? If you're the one doing the shopping and the cooking you are in control of what is in your fridge or larder.

I hope you all have room for dessert because I made your favourite – store bought snack cakes, both kinds.

Marge, *The Simpsons*

How involved are your children in the family's shopping and cooking? At what age do you think they need to start learning how to cook? Studies show that children are far more likely to try different foods if they have helped to prepare and cook them. With babies, expose them to a wide range of tastes and don't give up when they spit something out. Apparently, you need to try something ten times before you know if you like it or not.

Top tip

Encourage your children to help with shopping, cooking, serving and clearing up. Aim for a ten year old to be able to cook a meal once a week. Pasta and a jar of sauce is fine; the point is, to involve them in food and nutrition. You can thank them for their efforts and they will feel good about themselves too.

Don't expect schools to teach them how to cook.

Is your home a haven?

Ah! There is nothing like staying at home for real comfort.

Jane Austen, *Emma*

Does you home help you to be a mother? Is your home a comfortable haven or does it leave you tearing your hair out because nothing is where you want it to be and you just don't know where to start to give it a makeover? When it comes to tidying up, does everything have its place, or do you shove things in baskets and cupboards telling yourself you'll sort it out later? Are there a number of items around your home that need repairing? A leaky tap or a lightbulb to replace? Drafty doors, cracked tiles or broken toys? Weeds in the garden?

They may seem small jobs, but they are difficult to ignore and someone has to make the decision about fixing, replacing or discarding them. In your family, how easy is it for your children to tidy up or find things? If you ask your children to tidy up their bedroom, do they think that means stuffing things under their bed?

How you arrange your home environment is entirely up to you and your family, but if your home is creating problems for you (like increased levels of anxiety and bad temper) then would it be a good idea to have a rethink? Some very simple ideas can make a big difference.

I was often nagging at my four and six year olds to hang up their coats, and I am ashamed to say it took me ages to notice that they couldn't reach the coat pegs. There is a row of pegs at their height now, which will still be useful for scarves and bags when they're taller than me!

Laura, two children

If you would like to give your home a makeover to make it easier and more pleasing to live in, take time to work out what you would change and when you can do it. It can be overwhelming if you feel like the whole house is a nightmare, so the trick is to tackle one part at a time. Imagine how good it would be if you made those changes and the benefits it would create for you and the family.

Give your home a makeover – room by room

You will need about 20 minutes to complete the next exercise and a large piece of paper, at least A4 size.

Go in to each area of your home. What is really frustrating for you about that room? Is the tap dripping in the kitchen or the fridge resembling a biology project? Are the storage containers for the toys the wrong size for your toddler's bedroom? Is the blind in the baby's room broken? Are the bathroom tiles mouldy? Is your bedroom dull and functional? Is the garden (if you have one) a jungle of weeds? Is the living room arranged around the television as if that is the most important thing in the house? These are only ideas to get you thinking – this needs to be about *your* house and you need to think what *you* want to fix to make it work better for *you*.

I'm sitting on the toilet and I'm looking at the grouting on the tiles. That grouting really gets me. Mothers have a thing about grouting.

Sharon Osbourne

Making achievable, positive plans is vital, and remember to put aside a date and time to make these plans happen. This does not want to be just a nice dream on piece of paper which is ignored and is depressing when you eventually put it in the recycling bin. This needs to be an inspiring and realistic plan of action. What other resources will you need as well as time and money?

It could be worth investing in a babysitter for a couple of hours so you can sort out the children's bedrooms in the run up to

Christmas, or if your sister is brilliant at sorting out cupboards maybe she could do yours and you could do hers – other people's mess is much easier to tackle than your own!

You can draw up a table like the one below, or use a wheel or a mind map – whatever works for you.

Room or area	What the problems are	What I can do about them	What I will do and when
Kitchen	Food cupboards a mess. Nowhere to keep plastic containers. Toaster broken.	Sort/tidy food cupboards. Sort plastics out and recycle or create space to keep. Buy a new toaster.	Sunday afternoon – food cupboard and plastics – get kids to help or Jim to take them out. Buy toaster Tuesday – online if no time to shop.
Kid's bedroom	Biggest problem is their clothes – winter and summer all mixed up. No idea what still fits. Clothes dumped on the floor, not put away.	While they're at school 'weed' out really grotty or outgrown things. Buy more hangers and un-jam the sock drawer.	Saturday – put out everything that's left on the floor and sort out with them into 'keep', 'charity', or 'bin' piles. Show them how to fold tops and pair socks. Fix drawer.

Aim to target one room within the coming week. When is the best time to do these tasks? When you have chosen your room or area, what would be the best part to tackle first? What would keep you going and inspire you to tackle the next area? If possible, ask for help from your children and your partner. Make it fun, play some upbeat music, have a race to see who can find the missing sock or give the most to charity (within reason)!

In every job that must be done, there is an element of fun. You find the fun and snap! The job's a game...

Mary Poppins

You might find Mary Poppins' approach to tidying up irritating. However, moaning about a tidy-up session only drags you down, and it doesn't get the jobs done. By being positive and focusing on the benefits, your children learn that taking care of possessions and being able to find things when needed will help all of you to enjoy your home environment and make it easier to live in.

Imagine each space being a peaceful haven, free of clutter instead of a huge energy drain. Life outside the home is often stressful and chaotic enough, and coming home to a messy disorganized house is the last thing anyone wants to face after a hard day at work and school. You might not think it matters, but does everyone in the family feel that way? Nobody wants to live in a museum or feel like a war will break out because they used the last bit of toilet paper without writing it on the shopping list, but it *is* worth considering what could be done to make your home run better for you and your family. Mothers who know where to find things and pass this skill on to their children probably shout a bit less than mothers who don't.

Nothing stays the same

It will be gone before you know it. The fingerprints on the wall will appear higher and higher and then they will disappear.

Dorothy Evslin

Wherever you are on the path of motherhood you will know that you are on a journey and standing still is not an option. Children develop on every level at a very fast pace in the first ten years. You will find yourself saying clichés like 'They grow up so fast' or 'I can't believe he's starting school already'. Your first baby is likely to be the one that surprises and challenges you the most at every stage because you haven't had a baby, a two year old or a ten year old before. Even though your next child could be a very different personality, each stage they go through will have an element of familiarity about it. Remember, siblings thrive when their uniqueness is valued and upheld and just because you have been through the toddler years with your first child doesn't mean it will be exactly the same with the next one.

As well as your children being individuals, you are not quite the same mother either. You are getting older, a bit wiser, maybe a bit more relaxed. Perhaps you are alone, in a new relationship, or you are no longer working or have gone back to work. What other events will leave their mark on your path through motherhood?

The first ten years are about getting the hang of parenting in preparation for gradually launching your children into the world of adolescence and adulthood. Shortly before adolescence, mothers notice that their child is sometimes neither a child nor a teenager, but somewhere in between. There is a murky time in child development that arrives around the age of eight and lasts until they are about 12 years old. You might find your child moody and rebellious one minute, and wanting lots of cuddles and hot chocolate with you the next. Some parents feel they are already living with a teenager but that is not the case, the challenges and joys of adolescence are to follow. Living with these changes can be hurtful and bewildering if your child has overtaken your readiness to let them grow up a bit.

Being a mother and running a family is like spinning plates. Just when you think you are on top of things something happens and the family changes again. Someone has a birthday, or a baby is born, or someone hits a rough patch and one or more of your plates are wobbling again. Families have always been like this, so embrace the change rather than fearing it, and just do what you can to get that plate spinning again.

Anon

Thinking about your family now, how do you feel about dealing with the changes as your children grow up?

What will you find challenging about your children growing up?

What will be the joys?

Do you know a family who has coped well with the changes? What is it you admire about them?

Wouldn't it be boring if one year was much the same as the next?

You will be running a home and family for at least 20 years, until your last child leaves home. Motherhood is not something that ends when your child turns 18. More children are taking longer to leave home as they cannot afford to, relationships break down or jobs are lost and they have no choice but to return home.

If you doubt your ability to be a good mother, then have faith in the fact that you will learn as you go along, and remember that perfection is not the aim. You will do the best you can with each child at each stage. Motherhood is a brilliant job for life – you are already, and always will be, good enough.

Motherhood is like your bra. Close to your heart and there for support.

Anon

Learning log

Check you are happy that you have learnt each point below and feel ready to apply it to your life.

- Appreciate the different ingredients needed to run your family.
- Know how to get on top of daily family life.
- Consider family feelings and needs.
- Do a health check – is it wine and TV or herbal tea and a jog that you choose?
- Make your job as a mother easier by improving your home environment.
- Understand the changes that will occur as children grow older.

What have I learnt about myself as a mother by reading this chapter?

What is the most significant thing?

10

enjoy being a mum, create a happy family

In this chapter you will learn:
- what creates a happy childhood
- what constitutes a fun mum
- how to celebrate special occasions
- the importance of investing in fun.

My mum is nice to sit on. She's all soft and nice and bouncy.

Daniel, 11 years old

Imagine it's your seventieth birthday party. Your family and friends have gathered to celebrate with you. Your children have long since grown up (they're about the age you are now) and perhaps they have children of their own. The party is in full swing, and it's time to cut the cake. Your children start to pay tribute to you as their mother.

What are they saying about you?

What are they sharing of their childhood memories?

Sitting here now, reading this book, what do you hope they will be saying?

Although your seventieth birthday party might feel like a long way off when you're thinking about fish fingers for tea and what time to pick up your toddler, this is a great question to invest some time in answering. Most parents hope their children will look back on their childhood as happy one. The part mothers have to play in creating happy childhoods is huge, but instead of being daunted, seize this opportunity to learn about what helps to create that happy childhood. Where will you create that sense of fun and enjoyment you hope your children will remember about their early years?

So, let's start with those twilight years in mind... go back to the party for a minute.

The wheel of hope and happiness

In an ideal world, what *do* you hope your children will remember about their childhood? Fill in your children's happiness wheel here with eight positive things you want them to remember. One mum's happiness wheel contained the words Love, Security, Fun, Affection, Calm, Creativity, Joy and Laughter. Choose the words you would like.

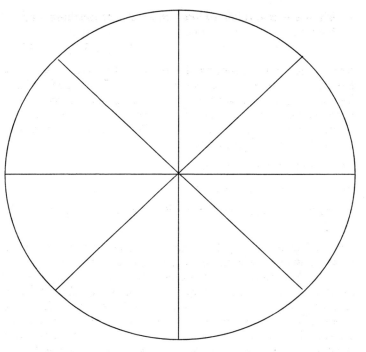

Now, pick out your top three hopes here – the ones that you can't do without.

I hope that my children will remember their childhoods as...

1.

2.

3.

Imagine having a childhood like that? By having these positive values lived out in their childhood, how will that serve your children in their adult lives?

If they have children, how will this influence their own parenting?

The good news is that you can give these values to your children. You probably already are, but is there room for improvement?

Let's start by making good use of our own memories.

Resurrecting your own childhood

I want my children to have a childhood similar to mine...

A recent survey by Mind Lab (researcher David Lewis, *Daily Mail*, 24 July 2007) revealed that many adults have vivid happy childhood memories of things like making sandcastles, daisy chains or flying kites. The danger is that today's children are missing out on these simple pleasures and spending too much time in front of computers and TVs. Parents are very busy, and finding time to be completely focused on playing with children is difficult. We know it's important to give children some freedom to experiment. It would be good to develop the art of risk taking, but how do we do that when the world is a dangerous place?

Lots of mums have happy memories of their childhood which they want to recreate for their own children. The chances are, most of these happy moments had something to do with an adult being there, or having created the opportunity for you.

My mum had endless patience; she would let us play at the sink for hours, making a terrible mess now I come to think about it, but she never complained. We had a great time destroying tea bags and pouring out imaginary cups of tea for her.

June, mother of three

Maybe you can remember playing outside in the sunshine for hours. You might have been alone, but somewhere in the background was there a parent who cared about you enough to give you the freedom to play unsupervised and who trusted you would be okay?

Thinking back to when you were a child, what three happy memories stand out?

Describe three happy memories of your childhood here...

1.

2.

3.

Now answer these questions:

What was the feeling you remember most from each of these memories?

(e.g. happiness, excitement, pleasure, love, security, freedom)

How does it make you feel now remembering these stories?

Sometimes we can feel sad when we are reminded of happy times in our childhood. It can bring up feelings of loss or disappointment in the parenting we received. It can also remind us of what was good about our parents if you find it hard to think positively about them.

Looking at what you have written about your happy childhood memories, is there something you would like to bring into your own children's lives that's been missing or neglected? Is it a feeling (e.g. freedom)? Is it an activity (e.g. this has made me aware that my children don't play outside enough)?

What was your own mother like?

This might be hard for you to think about if you have or had a difficult relationship with your own mother or she has passed away. What we cannot avoid is that the style of mothering we received will inform how we mother our own children. Sometimes understanding what it was like for our mothers at the time can help *us* to understand and forgive the parts of their mothering that we prefer to forget.

I never really understood my mother until I had kids of my own.

Anon

If you would like to, think about some happy times in your childhood with your own mother. If that's uncomfortable or painful, or you can't remember, can you think of some other happy childhood memories with a different adult?

I remember being tucked up in bed at night and my mum squeezing me tight as she said goodnight. Sometimes she had perfume on if they were going out. I loved that squeeze from her – I felt safe and happy which was a lovely feeling to have as I went off to sleep.

Laura, mother of three

Happy memories I have about being with my mother...

1.

2.

Can you remember any other mothers of your childhood friends or family that were positive, fun and/or enjoyable to be with? What were the reasons for this?

Write them here (e.g. I remember my friend's mother always made me feel very welcome by asking if I would like to stay for supper).

Other mums or adults who made me feel happy/special/welcome...

Their name(s)...

What they did that gave me this feeling...

It's common to wish your mother could be more like someone else's mother. If you feel like that, it can help to recognize that most mothers were doing the best they could with what resources they had. They cobbled together parenting ideas from the way they were raised and by chatting with neighbours, family and friends. They probably didn't buy books about parenting or go on parenting courses, but in their own way they too were hoping our childhoods were happy.

Enjoying family life

What does it mean to enjoy family life?

Everyone's answer to this could be different. For some it might just mean peace and quiet, a day without having a row. For other mothers it could be a feeling that everything in your family is sailing along nicely without needing to add anything extra. Maybe it means playing a board game together for hours on a wet Sunday afternoon. Or having a barbeque with friends – the point is, what does enjoying family life mean to you? Once you know what it means to you, you can start building on ways to bring more enjoyment and happiness in, but firstly, let's do a reality check.

How much fun is your family having?

Before you can make changes to bring some more enjoyment into the family, it's a good idea to have a play around on the 'fun-o-meter' with the stars scoring system to see how much fun is going on at the moment.

The examples shown are from lots of families who have found ways to enjoy family life. (There is space at the bottom for you to add in your own ideas too.)

The star scoring system

* 1 star – we hardly ever do this (less than once a month)
** 2 stars – we sometimes do this (about once a week)
*** 3 stars – we often do this (every day)

Simply tick the column that applies:

Idea	1 star *	2 stars **	3 stars ***
Enjoy a family meal together			
Play a game together			
Enjoy an outing together			
Play a sport together			
Go for a walk or bike ride			
Dance together			
Watch TV together			
Share an activity – art, DIY, cooking			
Read a story together			
Laugh together			
Willingly help each other			
Enjoy a special occasion – e.g. birthday			
Tickle or play fight each other			
Add your ideas here...			

Count up your stars. What's your total?

12–24 = Time to inject some more enjoyment into your family.

24–34 = You're doing well, but there's room for improvement to crank up the enjoyment.

35 or more = It sounds like you have loads of fun together – keep it up!

Share the joy

Looking at your star score, are there some things you would like to do to boost the fun factor in your family? Does it have to be you? Can your partner help out here – if so, when can you have a conversation with him about what he can offer? Best of all, involve your children. They are often the experts at coming up with fun ideas. Make sure you are clear about a budget or the time available though. Also, siblings, what could they do together that would be enjoyable for them? Spread the load, it's not just your job to bring enjoyment into the family.

Make a list here of everyone else who can share the task of bringing enjoyment to your family, and what is their particular gift. For example, maybe your sister is really keen to take your daughters shopping, or your neighbour has a big paddling pool she has offered to lend you. If you have a baby, is there a toy library or a charity shop where you could find new toys? Where could you go to meet other mothers with little ones? Think of five other people who can bring in more joy to your family.

Who can add joy? What is their gift?

1.

2.

3.

4.

5.

Do you feel slightly less responsible now for being the main creator of fun in the family? Maybe you're the kind of mother who would like to think of ways to boost the fun as it's usually someone else who does this? What can you do over the next seven days to increase your star score? Think of one thing to do each day – make it something easy, simple and free of charge if possible. Also, it's important that you'll enjoy it too – what's the point in setting up a game of snakes and ladders if you keep looking at your watch or answering the phone? Your children can spot instantly if you're pretending to enjoy something. It can help if you focus on their enjoyment rather than your own thoughts and feelings.

To be honest, I loathe playing chasing games in the garden with my daughter Sophie, but I know she loves it. I dread her asking me, as I can't help noticing all the jobs that need doing in the garden when I'm out there. I usually haven't got the energy to run about, and quite frankly, I would prefer to put my feet up with a magazine. One Sunday afternoon, my parents came over and helped do some weeding, and surprisingly, I felt more able to play chase at the same time with Sophie – I didn't notice the time passing and I looked such a sweaty mess at the end of if, but Sophie was so happy I just didn't care, it was great!

Eleanor, two children

This mum was fortunate enough to have her parents' support. If you are on your own, it might be harder to get the support you need to spend time playing with your children. Choose to make it a priority as often as possible. Even five minutes spent cuddling and laughing together will keep you all going for a long time. Your children won't always be with you but chores will.

Boost your family fun this week	
	What I will do
Monday	
Tuesday	
Wednesday	
Thursday	
Friday	
Saturday	
Sunday	

Excellent! You have made a great commitment to your family to increase the fun factor this coming week. What that shows is that you *are* a fun mum who has just come up with seven great ideas to bring more fun into your family. Well done!

Creating fun mums

Earlier, we were considering who we remember from our past that was a great mother and what were the qualities we associated with her. It might be our own mother, or someone from our childhood who was a joy to be around and made us feel good about ourselves. Use those memories to inspire you, not to make you feel inadequate or guilty. When we compare ourselves to other mothers we can feel worse, and our confidence takes a big knock.

The other mums at the school gate seem more cheerful and relaxed than me. I just can't seem to be like that, and I'm always worrying about the next thing which is no good for me, or my daughter.

Laura, two children

Instead of comparing yourself to other mothers, what can you learn from them and apply to your life? Focus on being the kind of mum you *want* to be instead of feeling hurt, resentful, a failure or no good. Don't tell yourself that everyone else seems to be better at being a mother than you are.

Reinforcing these negative ideas about yourself is not helpful to you, and your children will notice the effect this has on you. They are experts at picking up on our moods and feelings from a very young age.

Have a go at writing here some ideas about the qualities you admire in other mothers – what is it about them? What do they do? Be inspired by this and adapt it to your own style.

Qualities of a mother

Idea 1. What is it about this idea that inspires you?

Idea 2.

Idea 3.

There's a mum I know who always bakes her kids amazing birthday cakes. My baking skills are hopeless so I buy a cake, but I would feel better about it if I could make one. However, this year I decided to buy a plain cake and some icing kits and I had a go. I felt really proud of myself, and my son thought it was great – maybe next year I might try baking it too!

Jane, two children

What stops you having fun with your children?

Elizabeth is a full-time mum with two children, aged seven and four. She is at home every day with them, and she resents the endless amount of mess the kids make by getting out games and toys and not putting them away. She realized that she was wearing herself out tidying up several times a day and feeling resentful about this too. It was making her irritable, and more likely to shout at the children. She wanted to reduce her anxiety about keeping the house tidy, and at the same time create ways to have more fun with the children. Before she could do this, it was important to be clear about what was getting in the way of her being able to relax and make time to enjoy her children a priority. Elizabeth isn't the only mum who feels like this.

A group of mothers on a parenting workshop came up with the following answers to the question 'What stops you having fun with your children?'

- 'I can't let myself go when there are jobs to do.'
- 'I don't enjoy children's games.'

- 'I'm too tired.'
- 'I haven't got time to play.'
- 'However much I play with them is never enough.'
- 'I need to make some phone calls or send e-mails while the kids are occupied.'
- 'My mum never played with us – she was always too busy.'
- 'They just want to play on the computer and those games are mind-boggling to me.'
- 'I feel reluctant to join in as they will keep asking me to play and be less keen to play without me.'
- 'My toddler just comes and destroys what I'm doing with my older son.'
- 'The phone is always ringing.'
- 'I just can't be bothered sometimes.'
- 'I don't see the need when my husband is always happy to play with them – he's so good at it.'

Are you one of those mums who finds it hard to let go and make having fun with your children a priority? Or do you start playing with them and then stop when the phone goes? Or do you feel you're not really any good at playing with them?

Identify what will get in the way of you playing with your children.

What are the five biggest challenges that stop you having fun and enjoying your children?

1.

2.

3.

4.

5.

Looking at your answers, what do you learn about yourself as a mother? Which challenge would you *most* like to do something about?

If you could sort out that challenge (e.g. if you wrote that you were 'too tired', you could find a way to boost your energy levels) what would the benefit be to you, your children and your partner?

What would have to be in place to make it possible to deal with that challenge (e.g. to go to bed half an hour earlier on week nights to get more sleep)?

What would you need to believe about yourself in order to make this easy? (Only write this in positive language, e.g. I am an energetic mother and I will make boosting my energy levels a priority.)

This week, write out your new belief about your challenge and keep it where you can see it and say it aloud to yourself every day. Keep a note every time you experience this belief coming to life – for example making time to get more sleep.

Remember… what stops you now might change over time. You might feel differently when your children are older, for instance. You might find it easier to play with one of your children than another. One mother found her older son was a delight to kick a football around with, whereas the other one was too rough and competitive and she dreaded having to play with him. This led to feelings of guilt, and it was easier to just avoid playing football with either of them, which led to more guilt. If this is true for you, then see if you can turn that guilt off as it's a huge energy drain and what good is that to you or your children? Focus instead on the fact that being aware of this difference in your children is the first step towards doing something about it.

Take action

What will you do about your biggest challenge that stops you having fun with your children?

My first step is...

When will I do this...

Well done – you have learnt what stops you having fun with your children, and what you want to do about it. Will you do it?

Now, back to Elizabeth... Instead of assuming that life with young children would just carry on being tiring, messy, chaotic and irritating, Elizabeth decided she could take some action and reinvent herself as a mother who was capable of enjoying her children and feeling good about herself. Using the fun mum wheel exercise on the next page, she came up with eight new actions to boost her fun mum factor.

1 Tidy up once a day and involve the children in this.
2 Make a new rule with them that they must put away a game first before getting the next out – make this a race, not a shouted instruction.
3 Play with them at least once a day.
4 Commit to banishing gloomy thoughts (e.g. 'This is a waste of time, I ought to be getting tea ready') while playing with them and focus instead on enjoying them.
5 Arrange for some 'Me' time – ask a friend to swap children once a week for a couple of hours.
6 Plan a nice outing with the family once month and book it.
7 Create a wall chart for the week so everyone can see when they have good things to look forward to, not just muddle along from day to day.
8 See the mess as evidence of a happy busy family that I am lucky to have.

When Elizabeth looked at her wheel, the option that appealed to her most was to plan an outing that she thought would give all the family something to look forward to. They went on a camping weekend and they all had a fantastic time. She also made a decision to no longer see the mess as a pain, but to accept it as a sign of a happy and busy family, and clearing up once a day was good enough. She also invested in some bright storage bins and explained to the children how to use them to store their toys, making tidying up even easier.

The fun mum wheel

So what would your fun mum wheel look like? In the fun mum wheel, choose eight ways to bring more fun and enjoyment into your life. Make sure they are realistic and within your control – *and* exciting and appealing to you – think of something you haven't done before or for a long time. Be daring and adventurous! This is your path towards being the kind of mother you want to be.

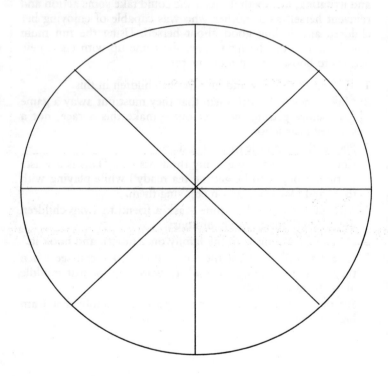

Top three activities in your wheel that you would like to do most...

1.

2.

3.

What is it about these three that appeals to you?

What do you need to do to bring these three ideas to life?

When will you start?

Is there anything that will stop you?

Top tip

Be a family that has fun for free!

Festivals and celebrations

Christmas time. Children are at home and the excitement is mounting as they look forward to Christmas morning and tearing open their presents. The house is warm and the smells of festive cooking ooze from the kitchen making tummies rumble. The high streets are crowded with last-minute anxious shoppers clutching lists and hoping their credit cards will take the strain. Where are the mothers in this frantic last few days before families retreat inside and the holidays begin? What is it like in your home in the run up to Christmas?

Mothers will be at the heart of what it takes for a family to celebrate. Whether it's Christmas, a birthday or any other special occasion, the organizing and doing will be in the hands of mothers in most families. It's an exceptional mother who sails through a Christmas or a birthday in the family without feeling overwhelmed or stressed at some point. It's easy to spend too much, eat and drink too much and feel that your children's values about special occasions are far from ideal. Children are much more interested in receiving rather than giving. They are bombarded by TV commercials for toys which will then be repeated to you at every opportunity. Lists are carefully written for Santa and for their birthdays, and on the day itself your little angels will rip through one present after the another, hardly noticing what's inside. But it's still up to the grown ups in the family (that includes you) to set the tone about how these special occasions are going to be celebrated. If you dread Christmas and/or birthdays, is it because you feel out of control and swamped by them, which leaves you stressed and anxious? Think about how you want your children to look back on their childhood Christmases and birthdays. Decide with your partner what you *really* want these occasions to be like, instead of getting sucked into a vortex of spending and overindulging.

If you're in the mood, take some time now (even if it's a boiling hot summer's evening) to do some thinking about Christmas or the next birthday so you can make some good choices about it for you and the family. If not now, you could write a date in your diary when you could do this.

Whether it's Christmas or a birthday or some other special occasion, here are the basic ingredients that are usually on a mother's To Do list:

- Food – planning, shopping, cooking, dealing with leftovers
- Drinks – alcoholic and non alcoholic, glasses and ice
- Cards – buying, writing, sending
- Presents – planning, budgeting, shopping, wrapping, posting
- Event (e.g. a party) – planning, budgeting, shopping, hosting
- Visitors – who to see, where and when
- House – is it ready? Make the beds, clean and tidy, put decorations up, garden usable, plenty of basic things in stock (even loo roll)
- Money – how much to spend (or just spend and hope for the best?)
- Going away – booking travel plans, packing, pet care, security
- Afterwards – thank you letters, finding homes for new things, eat bread and drink water for a week!

What else would be on your list? Looking at this list, how much of it are you in control of? How much of it leaves you feeling overwhelmed? Are you really the only person in the family who has to do everything?

Your first step to making these occasions easier and more enjoyable is to write around the candle below (a universal symbol of light and hope) your ideal way to celebrate a special occasion as a family. What would be important to you? Think about what you want your children to remember about these key events in childhood. Place the major themes around the candle, or use the list above to help you think of all the different aspects that are important to you.

Special days in your family

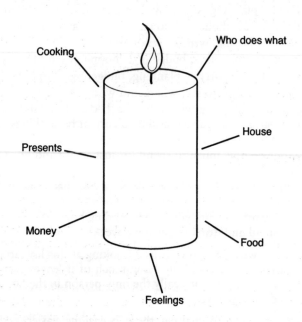

It's up to you to review what you have written around the candle and update it over the coming years. Your family milestones deserve to be treasured memories, not disasters you would prefer to forget.

Investing in fun

Has this chapter got you thinking about the value of having more opportunities to enjoy your family and being a mother? Yes, there are always distractions to put you off investing in time to enjoy being a family, but hold on to what is really important to you and make that your priority. Imagine your children saying to you at your seventieth birthday party 'Mum had fun with us and we have loads of happy memories' (as well as 'Mum always made sure we were well fed and had clean clothes'). Both domestic care and happy experiences are bound up in motherhood, but what do you want to feature most in your children's memories?

As you learnt from Chapter 09, Running a family, there will never be enough hours in the day to get everything done – so why keep trying when you could invest time every day to enjoy your children? You have choices here, and it is up to you to start being the kind of mother you want to be – everyone will benefit – most of all you.

Time's up...

This book began by inviting you to choose the order in which you read it, so it's hard to know if these are the last words you're reading. The intention has been to take you through the main features of motherhood in order to raise your awareness of what motherhood is about. No book could include every aspect of motherhood; it's far too complex and unique to each mother. Books, websites, TV programmes, family and friends will join you on your journey of learning about motherhood, but your greatest teachers will be your children. Before you realize it, the challenges and joys of adolescence will be with you. Remember, your children will be adults for far more years than they are children. One day there will be an empty laundry basket and the house will be a little too quiet. You will wonder if anyone will ever climb onto your lap again and whisper in your ear just how special you are. Treasure the first ten years with your children now; they will be over in a heartbeat.

A mother never realizes her children are no longer children.

Holbrook Jackson

Last learning log

Check you are happy that you have learnt each point below and feel ready to apply it to your life.

- Understand what creates a happy childhood.
- Know how to help our children to achieve this.
- Know how to be a fun mum.
- Measure the fun in your family, is there enough?
- Making special occasions exactly that.
- Investing your time and effort in fun.

What have I learnt about myself as a mother by reading this chapter?

What is the most significant thing?

A final recap

As this is the end of the book, please return to the introduction where you recorded your original goals for reading it.

Look at the scores you gave your knowledge for each chapter, how have your scores improved?

The three main areas that you wanted to learn about were:

1.

2.

3.

In what ways has your knowledge improved in these areas?

What has had the most significant impact on you?

Learning new ideas and changing habits takes time and energy. You have made a great investment in yourself as a mother. What can you do to protect and develop your learning?

Thank you for the time and effort you have given to read this book.

I would love to read your stories about how this book has helped you. You can contact me through my website **www.parentingpeople.co.uk.**

taking it further

Aren't we lucky to live in the twenty-first century and have a wealth of organizations, websites, charities and communities who can help us find out more?

Births and babies

The Association for Post Natal Illness (APNI)
145 Dawes Road
Fulham
London
SW6 7EB
Tel: 0207 386 0868.
www.apni.org

Andrea Grace
Baby sleep expert
www.andreagrace.co.uk

Breastfeeding Network
The Breastfeeding Network
PO Box 11126
Paisley
PA2 8YB
UK
Tel: 0844 41224664
www.breastfeedingnetwork.org.uk

Cry-sis
Phone line and help for parents with crying babies/children
Tel: 08451 228 669
www.cry-sis.org.uk

La Leche League
Mother to mother support and advice about breastfeeding
Tel: 0845 120 2910
www.laleche.org.uk

Meet a mum
Association and helpline for those feeling lonely or isolated after birth
Tel: 0845 1203746
www.mama.co.uk

National Childbirth Trust
For antenatal and postnatal classes, advice and support.
Tel: 0870 444 8709
www.nct.org.uk

Children's special needs

ADD/ADHD online support group
www.adders.org

Contact A Family
Comprehensive information for families with children with disabilities
Tel: 0808 808 3555
www.cafamily.org.uk

Twins and Multiple Birth Association
Tel: 0800 138 0509
www.tamba.org.uk

Childcare

Association of Nannies
www.anauk.org

British Au Pair Agencies Association
Trafalgar House
Grenville Place
London
NW7 3SA
Tel: 07946 149 916
www.bapaa.org.uk

Childcare Link
Government resource for national and local childcare
www.childcarelink.gov.uk
Tel: 0800 0960296

Children's Information Service
Offers information and guidelines on choosing childcare
www.childrensinformationservice.org.uk

National Childminding Association of England and Wales
Tel: 0845 880 0044
www.ncma.org.uk

The Parent Centre
Government information on many parenting aspects including childcare
www.parentscentre.gov.uk

Parenting support

BBC parenting website
Online parenting ideas and latest news
www.bbc.co.uk/parenting

Families online
Regional magazine and online parenting ideas
www.familiesonline.co.uk

Home Start
A national charity supporting families with one or more child under five
www.home-start.org.uk

Parentlineplus
National charity with free helpline, advice, courses and materials
Tel: 0808 800 2222
www.parentlineplus.org.uk

Parenting UK
National body for parenting education and information about parenting course providers
Tel: 0207 284 8370
www.parentinguk.org
www.practicalparent.org.uk

Parent Coaching
One to one support for parents by phone or in person
www.parentingpeople.co.uk
www.theparentcoachingacademy.co.uk

Raising Kids
Online support and advice
www.raisingkids.co.uk

Sure Start
Advice, support and parent centres for families nationwide
www.surestart.gov.uk

Gingerbread/One Parent Families
The association for lone parent families
Tel: 0800 018 5026
www.gingerbread.org.uk

Mothers or fathers groups

Websites:

www.mumsnet.com
www.netmums.com
www.forparentsbyparents.com
www.fathersdirect.com
www.homedad.org.uk

Working mums

Websites

Jobs advertised, advice and support

www.motheratwork.co.uk
www.workingmums.co.uk

Mum and working
Specializes in jobs and support for mothers who want to work part time
www.mumandworking.co.uk

Working families
Advice, legal information and jobs for parents
www.workingfamilies.org.uk

Health

Imperfectly Natural Woman
Ideas, tips and forum for being a greener parent
www.imperfectlynatural.com

NHS direct
24-hour helpline for medical advice
Tel: 0845 46 47
www.nhsdirect.nhs.uk

Relate
Counselling for relationships
www.relate.org.uk

Women's Aid
National organization to support victims of domestic violence
Tel: 0808 2000 247
www.womensaid.org.uk

Recommended reading

Anything that will cheer you up – a magazine and a glass of wine can be just as beneficial to mothers as any parenting book.

Back to work

Katz, A (1992) *The Juggling Act* UK, Bloomsbury
Wolfin, D and Foreman, S (2004) *Back to Work* UK, Robson Books

Parenting

Biddulph, S (1984) *The Secrets of Happy children* Australia, Harper Collins

(Any book by Steve Biddulph is worth reading)

Cleese, J and Skinner, R, (1983) *Families, and how to Survive them* UK, Manderin
Faber, A and Mazlich, E (1980) *How to Talk so Kids will Listen and Listen so Kids Will Talk* New York, Avon books
Faber, A and Mazlich E (1987) *Siblings without Rivalry,* USA W.W. Norton
Hayman, S (2005) *Stepfamilies* UK, Simon and Schuster
Lee Grace, J (2007) *Imperfectly Natural Baby and Toddler* UK, Orion
Maushart, S (1999) *The Mask of Motherhood* UK, Pandora
Purves, L (1986) *How not to be a Perfect Mother* UK, Montana
Parker, J and Stimpson, J (1999) *Raising Happy Children* UK, Hodder and Stoughton
Parsons, R (2000) *The Sixty Minute Mother* UK, Hodder and Stoughton
Rattle, A and Vale, A (2006) *A Mother's Wit* UK, Prion

Self help/Coaching

Covey, S R (1988*) The 7 Habits of Highly Effective Families* UK, Simon and Schuster
Harrold, F (2000) *Be Your Own Life Coach* UK, Hodder and Stoughton
Thomas, L, (2005) *The 7 Day Parent Coach* UK, Vermillion
Thomas, L (2006) *Screamer to Sweet Dreamer* UK, Hodder Arnold

index